The Cambridge
Mathematics
Dictionary
for Schools

PRAESA
Karen Press

CAMBRIDGE
UNIVERSITY PRESS

CAMBRIDGE
UNIVERSITY PRESS

University Printing House, Cambridge CB2 8BS, United Kingdom

One Liberty Plaza, 20th Floor, New York, NY 10006, USA

477 Williamstown Road, Port Melbourne, VIC 3207, Australia

314–321, 3rd Floor, Plot 3, Splendor Forum, Jasola District Centre, New Delhi – 110025, India

79 Anson Road, #06–04/06, Singapore 079906

The Water Club, Beach Road, Granger Bay, Cape Town 8005, South Africa

Cambridge University Press is part of the University of Cambridge.

It furthers the University's mission by disseminating knowledge in the pursuit of education, learning and research at the highest international levels of excellence.

www.cambridge.org
Information on this title: www.cambridge.org/9780521708821
© Cambridge University Press 2008

First published 2008
20 19 18 17 16 15 14 13 12 11 10 9 8

Printed in South Africa by Academic Press

ISBN 978-0-521-70882-1 paperback

Editors: Erna du Toit, Christine de Nobrega
Typesetter: A1 Graphics
Illustrators: Sue Beattie, Robin McBride, Terence O'Hara and Anne Evans

Project ID: 32564

. . . .

Acknowledgements

Welma Odendaal – for cover photographs

A Mathematical Dictionary for Schools by Brian Bolt and David Hobbs, Cambridge University Press, 1998 – for graphics on pages 25 (conic section), 50 (fractal), 52 (glide reflection), 73 (mapping), 116 (rotation, first image), 143 (varies directly as), 144 (varies inversely as).

. . . .

If you want to know more about this book or any other Cambridge University Press publication, phone us at (021) 412-7800, fax us at (021) 419-8418 or send an e-mail to capetown@cambridge.org

Foreword

This important reference tool for the classroom and for homework is aimed at both mother tongue and additional language speakers.

The Cambridge Mathematics Dictionary for Schools will assist learners to understand the most important mathematical terms, words, phrases and theorems, and will guide them in their understanding of the unique and specific language of mathematics.

Up-to-date terminology and easy-to-understand definitions are supported by example sentences that place headwords in a real-life context as well as by cross-references to similar or related terms.

Illustrations not only add extra value by visually conveying the meanings of certain definitions, but also help define the more abstract concepts by providing interesting visual interpretations.

Tables that are mentioned in the definitions have been placed together for easy access at the back of the dictionary. They include:
- different calendars
- the Morse code alphabet
- Roman numerals
- multiplication tables
- the multiplication square
- conversion tables for length, area, mass, volume, temperature, and clothing and shoe sizes
- seven base units of the SI system
- 12- and 24-hour time
- formulae for plane shapes and solids.

How to use the dictionary

The first and last headword on each double-page spread appears at the top left and right of every spread.

The headword is in colour to make it easy to find.

R

radius   A *radius* of a circle is any straight line drawn from the centre of the circle to a point on its circumference. The plural of *radius* is 'radii'.
• The *radius* of a bicycle wheel is found by measuring the length of any of its radii.

The definition explains the headword in easy-to-understand language.

Examples are given of headwords, by using everyday situations and placing the word in context.

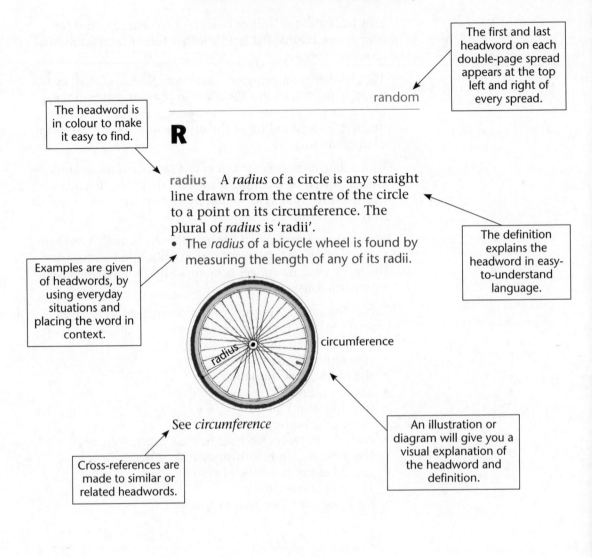

circumference

See *circumference*

Cross-references are made to similar or related headwords.

An illustration or diagram will give you a visual explanation of the headword and definition.

A

abacus   A frame with sliding beads on rods. It is used for doing arithmetic calculations.

- The calculation for this abacus is 1 ten plus 3 units = 10 + 3 = 13.

See *arithmetic*

abbreviation, abbreviate   An *abbreviation* is a shortened form of a word or group of words.
- We sometimes *abbreviate* the word 'kilogram' by writing 'kg'.

about   We use *about* to say that an amount is near to or close to another amount.
- The tree is *about* as tall as the house.

- There are *about* 1 000 beans in the packet – I haven't counted them exactly.

above   1. A thing is *above* something else if it is over it, or higher than it.
2. A number is *above* another number if it has a bigger value.

- The shelf is *above* the stove.

abstract   A thing is *abstract* if it has no form that we can see, hear, taste, smell or feel.
- Ideas and theories are *abstract* things that we think about.

acceleration, accelerate   *Acceleration* happens when the speed of a moving object increases. We usually calculate acceleration using the following formula:

$$\frac{\text{change of speed}}{\text{time it takes for speed to change}}$$

- A bicycle is travelling at 5 metres per minute. The cyclist increases speed to 11 metres per minute over 3 minutes. The bicycle's *acceleration* is:

$$\frac{\text{change of speed}}{\text{time it takes for speed to change}}$$

$$= \frac{11 - 5}{3}$$

= 2 (metres per minute) per minute or 2 metres per minute^2.

- New cars can *accelerate* faster than most older cars, because they have more powerful engines.

See *speed; velocity*

account   An *account* is a business record or statement that shows how much the customer must pay the business for goods or services she has bought.
- The school buys paper and pens from Supa Stationers. Every month Supa Stationers sends the school an *account* to show how much money it must pay.

SUPA STATIONERS	STATEMENT
Tel: (016) 424-7171 Fax: (016) 424-7172 www.supastationers.co.za email: supasta@iafrika.co.za	Date: 25/10/2020 Botshabelo Primary School Account Number: 1160

Botshabelo Primary School
15 High Street
Botshabelo
9781

Date	Reference	Description	Debit
25/08/2020	496482	15 reams of paper @ R43,00/ream	R645,00
25/08/2020	496483	37 ball point pens @ R3,75 each	R138,75
25/08/2020	496484	12 boxes of white chalk @ R5,35/box	R64,20
Amount Due:			R847,95

NEDBANK, HEIDELBERG
BRANCH CODE: 123 209
ACCOUNT NUMBER: 101 001 9988

accuracy of measurement When we count a set of objects, we get an exact number. But when we measure the mass, length or volume of something, we get a result that is not completely exact. The *accuracy of measurement* depends on how exact the measuring instrument is.
- A kitchen scale is not a very exact scale but it is accurate enough for baking. A chemist's scale has a better *accuracy of measurement* because it is important to get exact measurements for small masses of medicine.

See *accurate; measurement*

accurate 1. A statement is *accurate* if it tells the complete truth, without mistakes or lies.
2. A calculation is *accurate* if it gives you the exactly correct value of the answer.

See *accuracy of measurement*

acre An *acre* is equal to 4 840 square yards. It is part of the system of imperial units of measurement. One *acre* is equal to approximately 4 047 square metres.
- When African-American slaves were given their freedom in the USA, they were sometimes given a piece of land to farm that was about 40 *acres* big.

See *imperial units; metre*

across *Across* describes the direction in which something moves if it goes from one side to the other.
- The children walk *across* the road from the school gate to the bus stop.

activate To *activate* something means to make it start working or make it active.
- You *activate* a cell phone by pressing the button marked ①.

activity An *activity* is a project or exercise that you do to make something or learn about something. It usually consists of a group of step-by-step tasks.
- In a maths *activity*, the learners use their bodies to measure different lengths.

See *exercise*

acute angle An *acute angle* is an angle that is bigger than 0° and smaller than 90°.
- These are two examples of *acute angles*.

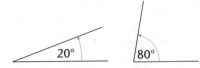

See *acute-angled triangle; angle*

acute-angled triangle An *acute-angled triangle* is a triangle in which all three angles are bigger than 0° and smaller than 90°.
- These triangles are both *acute-angled triangles*.

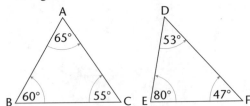

See *angle; triangle*

add To *add* things means to combine them together to get a total value. This total value is called the sum. We use the symbol + to indicate the instruction 'add'.
- If we *add* 3 and 5 we get the sum 8. We write it like this:
  $3 + 5 = 8$
- If we *add* 100 and 350 and 2 we get the sum 452. We write it like this:
  $100 + 350 + 2 = 452$

See *addition; plus; sum*

addition *Addition* is the general word we use to describe what we are doing when we add things together. We can also say *addition calculation* or *addition sums*.

See *add; calculation; sum*

additional   Something is *additional* if it is extra, or added on to what you already have.

- There are four wheels on this car. There is also an *additional* wheel. It is called the spare wheel.

additive inverse   The *additive inverse* of a number is the number that you add to it to get zero (0).

- The *additive inverse* of (+5) is (–5), because (+5) + (–5) = 0.
- The *additive inverse* of (–12) is (+12), because (–12) + (+12) = 0.

adjacent   Two things are *adjacent* if they are next to each other.

- The school and the clinic are *adjacent* on Bhunga Street.

See *adjacent angles*

adjacent angles   *Adjacent angles* are angles that share the same vertex and have one arm in common. They must lie on opposite sides of this common arm.

- Angles ABC and CBD are *adjacent angles*.

See *vertex*

adjacent sides   Two sides of a polygon are *adjacent* if they share a common vertex.

- In the square ABCD, AB and BC are *adjacent sides* because they share the vertex B.

- In the pentagon PQRST, QR and RS are *adjacent sides* because they share the vertex R.

See *pentagon; polygon; square; vertex*

after   We say that a number comes *after* another number if it comes behind it in the list or set of numbers.

- On this number line, 23 comes *after* 22.

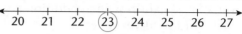

afternoon   The time between midday (12 o'clock) and evening (sunset) is called *afternoon*.

- School ends at two o'clock in the *afternoon* on weekdays.

See *p.m.*

algebra   *Algebra* is a branch of mathematics that uses letters and symbols to represent (stand for) numbers or other mathematical objects and to show the relationships between them. The word *algebra* comes from the Arabic words *al-jabr* (meaning putting together). Arabian mathematicians first developed *algebra* in about the 9th century. European mathematicians learned about *algebra* and developed it further during the following centuries. The letters and symbols used in *algebra*, and the rules for combining them, are called algebraic language.

- An example of *algebra* is the statement $a + b = c$. If we let $a = 10$ and $b = 5$, then c must be equal to 15. If we choose different number values for a and b, the value of c will be different.

See *algebraic expression*

algebraic expression   An *algebraic expression* is an expression (a combination of algebraic letters and symbols) in which the terms of the expression are separated from each other by + or – signs.

- $4a + 3b$ is an *algebraic expression* with two terms.
- $x^2 - 7xy + 2y^2$ is an *algebraic expression* with three terms.

algorithm   4

algorithm   An *algorithm* is a step-by-step method that you use to find the answer to a calculation. In mathematics, we learn different *algorithms* for different kinds of calculation such as addition, multiplication, division, etc.

- To find the highest common factor (HCF) of two numbers, for example 24 and 60, we can use an *algorithm* for finding highest common factors.
First express each number as a product of prime numbers:
$24 = 2 \times 2 \times 2 \times 3$
$60 = 2 \times 2 \times 3 \times 5$
Then find the prime factors that are common to both 24 and 60:
$2 \times 2 \times 3$
Then multiply these common prime factors together:
$2 \times 2 \times 3 = 12$
Therefore the HCF of 24 and 60 is 12.

See *highest common factor; prime number*

alphabet   An *alphabet* is a set of letters used in a language.

- The *alphabet* used in English, Sesotho, isiZulu and most other South African languages is:
a b c d e f g h i j k l m n o p q r s t u v w x y z

alternate angles   When a transversal line cuts two or more parallel lines, the angles on the opposite inside positions of the transversal are called *alternate angles*.

- In this diagram, the angles *s* and *t* are *alternate angles*.

See *parallel; transversal*

altitude of a triangle   In everyday English 'altitude' means 'height above sea level'. In mathematics, the *altitude of a triangle* is the length of a line drawn from one vertex of a triangle to meet the opposite side of the triangle at a right angle.

- In △ABC, the line AD is drawn from the vertex A to meet the line BC at a right angle (90°). AD is an *altitude of the triangle* ABC. You can also draw altitudes from B to meet AC, and from C to meet AB.
- The three *altitudes of a triangle* always pass through the same point. This point is called the orthocentre of the triangle.

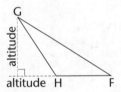

- In some triangles the altitude can fall outside the triangle itself. When the triangle is obtuse, two of the three altitudes, and the orthocentre, lie outside the triangle.

See *orthocentre; right-angled triangle; vertex*

a.m. (*ante meridiem*)   The letters *a.m.* stand for the Latin words *ante meridiem* which mean 'before noon'. We use these letters to describe the time between 12 o'clock midnight and 12 o'clock midday, on an analogue clock.

- The post office opens at 8.30 *a.m.* and closes at 4 p.m.

See *analogue clock; p.m.*

amount   An *amount* is a quantity of goods or material, or a number value.

- The *amount* of rice on the scale is 2 kg.
- In the subtraction sum below, the *amount* that is subtracted from 25 is 7:
$25 - 7 = 18$

analogue clock   An *analogue clock* is a clock that has a face with the numbers 1 to 12, and hands that move around the face to show the time. *Analogue clock* time is the time that you read off from the face of an *analogue clock*.

- This *analogue clock* face shows the time ten past three. From looking at this clock we cannot say whether this is ten past three in the early morning or ten past three in the afternoon.

See *a.m.; digital clock; p.m.*

angle   An *angle* is a measure of the amount of turning between two directions. The *angle* between two lines is the amount of turn needed to move one line until it lies on top of the other line. The two lines that form the *angle* are called the arms of the *angle*. The point where the arms meet is called the *vertex of the angle*.

- In the *angle* ABC the arrow shows the amount of turn that BC must make to lie on top of AB. This amount of turn is the size of the *angle*. *Angle* size is measured in degrees. The symbol for degrees is °.

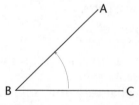

- On this analogue clock face, the minute hand turns through different *angles* to show the changing time.

At 3 o'clock the *angle* between the hour hand and the minute hand is 90°.

See *revolution; turn; vertex*

angle bisector   A line that divides an angle into two equal angles is called an *angle bisector*.

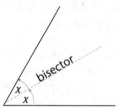

See *angle; bisect; bisector*

angle of depression   The *angle of depression* of an object is the amount of turn through which the eye has to move to look down at the object from a horizontal line above the object.

See *angle; horizontal*

angle of elevation   The *angle of elevation* of an object is the amount of turn through which the eye has to move to look up at the object from a horizontal line below the object. (This horizontal line is often the flat surface of the ground below the object.)

See *angle; horizontal*

anniversary   An *anniversary* is the date each year that marks an event that happened on the same date in a previous year. The celebration of this event is called an *anniversary celebration*.

- On 16 June 1976 the students of Soweto started an uprising to protest against apartheid education. Every year on 16 June we celebrate the *anniversary* of this uprising.
- The day that you call your 'birthday' is really the *anniversary* of your birthday. You can only have one real birthday in your life!

another *Another* comes from the two words 'an other'. *Another* object is an object that is different from an object we have already described. Or it can mean that we are adding an additional object.

answer The *answer* to a calculation or a problem is the solution that you have worked out. An *answer* is also a spoken or written reply to a question.
- The *answer* to the division calculation 125 ÷ 5 is 25.

See *calculation; problem*

anticlockwise An object turns *anticlockwise* if it turns in the opposite direction to the way the hands of an analogue clock turn.
- The ants are walking around the sugar bowl in an *anticlockwise* direction.

See *analogue clock; clockwise*

any *Any* means that it does not matter which one you choose from a group of objects.
- You can press *any* key on the computer to bring back the screen picture.

apex The *apex* of a shape is the top point of it – the point that is furthest away from the base of the object.

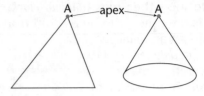

See *base*

applicable Something is *applicable* if it applies to a situation. In other words, it can be used in whatever you are doing at the time.
- The rules of rugby are not *applicable* to football. In rugby you are allowed to run with the ball, but in football this is not allowed.
- The rules for addition and subtraction are *applicable* to all positive and negative integers.

See *addition; integer; subtraction*

apportion To *apportion* something means to divide it into shares or parts, and to give each share or part to a different person or group. Each person or group gets a portion (part) of the whole.
- To *apportion* the farm fairly to 6 families we must divide the land into 6 equal parts.

See *equal; part; share*

appreciate 1. To *appreciate* something is to recognise its value.
2. In mathematical terms, something *appreciates* if its money value increases over time.
- My grandparents bought a house for R30 000 in 1982. Today they can sell it for R350 000. Its value has *appreciated* very much since 1982.

See *depreciate; increase; value*

approximate, approximately, approximation An *approximate* value is a value that is almost the same as the exact value to which it refers. We use an *approximate* value when we do not want to measure or calculate the value exactly. This is called *approximation*.

- The *approximate* number of people in South Africa is 46 million. It would be very hard to count all the people one by one, so we use this *approximation*.
- The distance from Johannesburg to Cape Town is *approximately* 1 400 kilometres. The exact distance depends on where you start driving from in Johannesburg, and where you stop your car in Cape Town when you get there.
- The sum of 343 and 62 is approximately 400. We get this *approximate* value by rounding off the two numbers before adding them.

See *round off*

approximation sign The *approximation sign* (≈) is used instead of the equal sign (=) to show that the answer to a calculation is not exact.

- $343 + 62 \approx 400$
- $520 \div 10 \approx 50$

See *equal sign*

arc of a circle An *arc of a circle* is any section of the circumference of a circle.

- In this circle, FG is an *arc* of the circle.
  PQ is also an *arc of* the circle.

See *circle; circumference*

arc of a network An *arc of a network* is any line (straight or curved) that joins two nodes of the network. In exceptional cases an arc may start and end at the same node.

- The network shown here has 3 arcs and 2 nodes.

See *network; node*

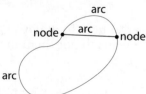

area The *area* of a place is the amount of space that it takes up. We use *area* to measure:

- the size of land regions such as provinces or countries;
- the size of smaller pieces of land such as a farm or a house plot;
- the size of flat objects such as pieces of paper.

We measure *area* with square units such as square centimetres (cm^2), square metres (m^2), hectares and square kilometres (km^2).

- The biggest province in South Africa is Northern Cape. It has an *area* of 361 830 km^2. The smallest province in South Africa is Gauteng. It has an *area* of 17 010 km^2.
- The *area* of this piece of cardboard is 12 square units.

See *square unit*

area formula We can calculate the area of certain types of shape by using an *area formula* for each shape.

- To calculate the area of a square we use the *area formula* side × side

- To calculate the area of a rectangle we use the *area formula* length × breadth

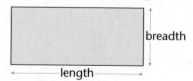

- To calculate the area of a parallelogram we use the *area formula* base × perpendicular height

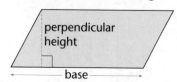

- To calculate the area of a triangle we use the *area formula*
  $\frac{1}{2}$ base × perpendicular height

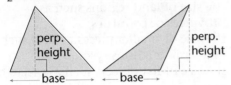

- To calculate the area of a trapezium we use the *area formula*
  $\frac{1}{2}$ (sum of parallel sides × perpendicular distance

  between parallel sides)

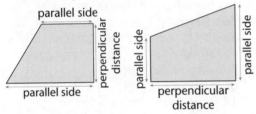

- To calculate the area of a circle we use the *area formula*
  $\pi(\text{radius})^2 = \pi r^2$

See *calculate; formula; parallel; perpendicular*

area under a graph   The *area under a graph* is the area between the horizontal axis of the graph and the line of the graph.
- In this graph the *area under the graph* is shaded.

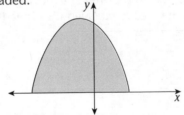

- In this graph the shaded area is the *area under the graph* from A to B.

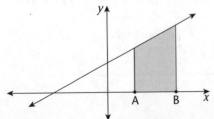

See *axis; graph; horizontal*

arithmetic   *Arithmetic* is the name for all the calculations you do with whole numbers, integers, fractions and decimal numbers. When you do addition, subtraction, multiplication and division with any of these numbers, you are doing *arithmetic*.
- $5\,000 + 175 = 5\,175$
  $25 \times 1{,}47 = 36{,}75$
  $\frac{3}{4} - \frac{2}{5} = \frac{7}{20}$
  $-25 \div +5 = -5$

See *addition; decimal; division; fraction; integer; multiplication; subtraction; whole number*

arithmetic technique   An *arithmetic technique* is a method that you use to do calculations with numbers.
- Addition, subtraction, multiplication and division are all examples of *arithmetic techniques*.

around   To go *around* something means to go along all the sides of it and come back to the place where you started. If you fly *around* the world, you are travelling in a complete circle that brings you back to your starting point.
- The fence goes *around* the field.
- The ribbon is tied *around* the ball.

arrange   To *arrange* a group of things means to put them in a certain order or pattern.
- If you *arrange* the numbers 3, 10, 7, 4, 2, 6, 1, 9, 5, 8 from smallest to biggest, you get: 1, 2, 3, 4, 5, 6, 7, 8, 9, 10.

- The learners *arranged* the chairs in a circle.

array   An *array* is a group of things arranged in a clear order or pattern.
- The numbers of learners in different age groups are shown in this *array*.

Age group	7-9	10-12	13-15	16-18	18-20
Number of learners	128	105	111	96	54

arrowhead   An *arrowhead* is a quadrilateral shape. It has two pairs of adjacent sides that are equal in length, and one of its interior angles is a reflex angle. The diagonal through the reflex angle is a line of symmetry for the *arrowhead*.

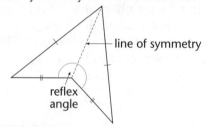
line of symmetry
reflex angle

See *adjacent sides; diagonal; interior angle; line of symmetry; quadrilateral; reflex angle*

ascend   To *ascend* means to go up.
- The lift *ascended* from the ground floor to the 25th floor.

See *descend*

ascending order   To arrange numbers in *ascending order* means to arrange them from the smallest number to the biggest number.
- If the numbers 25, 20, 30, 15, 5, 10 are arranged in *ascending order*, we get: 5, 10, 15, 20, 25, 30.

See *descending order*

associative property   An operation is associative if, when three elements are combined, it does not matter how the brackets that combine them are placed. In arithmetic, addition and multiplication are associative – they have the *associative property*. Subtraction and division do not have the *associative*

property because if you combine the elements in different ways, you get different answers.
- Addition has the *associative property* because:
$$(5 + 7) + 12 = 12 + 12 = 24$$
and $5 + (7 + 12) = 5 + 19 = 24$
so $(5 + 7) + 12 = 5 + (7 + 12)$
- Subtraction does not have the *associative property* because:
$$(20 - 12) - 4 = 8 - 4 = 4$$
and $20 - (12 - 4) = 20 - 8 = 12$
so $(20 - 12) - 4 \neq 20 - (12 - 4)$
- Multiplication has the *associative property* because:
$$(2 \times 3) \times 5 = 6 \times 5 = 30$$
and $2 \times (3 \times 5) = 2 \times 15 = 30$
so $(2 \times 3) \times 5 = 2 \times (3 \times 5)$
- Division does not have the *associative property* because:
$$(27 \div 9) \div 3 = 3 \div 3 = 1$$
and $27 \div (9 \div 3) = 27 \div 3 = 9$
so $(27 \div 9) \div 3 \neq 27 \div (9 \div 3)$

asterisk   The *asterisk* is the symbol *. 1. It can be used in printed books to link a word or sentence to another word or sentence somewhere else on the page, by placing an asterisk next to each. 2. It can be used as a way to refer to a group of things. 3. In mathematics, it can be used to stand for any operation that could be carried out on the numbers, for example $(a * b) * c = a * (b * c)$
- In this list of foods, the items marked with an asterisk all contain refined sugar: bread*; cheese; tomato sauce*; sausages; jam*; honey

asymmetric   A shape is *asymmetric* if it is not possible to draw any line of symmetry, which will divide the shape into two parts of the same size and shape.
- These shapes are *asymmetric*.

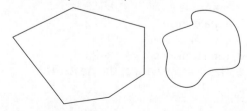

See *line of symmetry; symmetry*

autobank   An *autobank* is a machine that allows you to get money from your bank account or put money into the account without talking to a bank teller (the person who works at the bank). The *autobank* machine can also tell you what your account balance is. Another word for *autobank* is ATM (automated teller machine).

See *bank account; bank balance*

average   An *average* is a single number which is used to represent the general value of a collection of numbers or numerical information (data). There are different kinds of *averages*, such as the mean, the median and the mode. The mean is sometimes called the arithmetic mean.

- In her mid-year exams Thokozile receives these results:
  Mathematics 72%
  isiXhosa 69%
  Natural Sciences 73%
  Technology 64%
  Social Sciences 71%
  English 66%
  Economic and Management Sciences 57%
  Arts and Culture 60%
  Life Orientation 67%
  Her *average* result in the exams is:

$$\frac{(72 + 69 + 73 + 64 + 71 + 66 + 57 + 60 + 67)}{9}$$
$$= \frac{599}{9} = 66,5\%.$$

See *data; mean; median; mode*

average price   The *average price* of an item is the general price that you get if you compare the prices that different shops charge for that item.

- A gas heater is sold for these prices at different shops:

Home Heat	R350
SupaStores	R322
Discount Bazaar	R339
Top Furnishers	R425

  The *average price* of the heater is:

$$\frac{(350 + 322 + 339 + 425)}{4}$$
$$= \frac{1\,436}{4} = R359$$

average speed   The *average speed* for a journey is the total distance travelled, divided by the total time taken.

- When you drive from Johannesburg to Polokwane, you cover 296 km. If you travel for 4 hours, your *average speed* for the whole journey is 296 km ÷ 4 h = 74 km/h.

See *speed*

axis (plural: axes)   1. A graph usually has two *axes* – a horizontal *axis* and a vertical *axis*. The *axis* is a straight line showing the number values of the graph. 2. An *axis* is a straight line that goes through the centre of a 3-D object. The object can turn around this straight line.

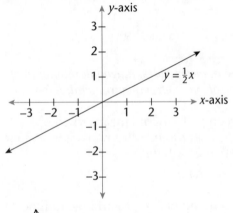

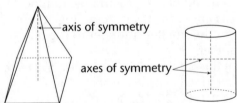

See *graph; horizontal; rotational symmetry; three-dimensional; vertical; x-axis; y-axis*

axis of symmetry   See *rotational symmetry*

B

baker's dozen A *dozen* is a collective name for a group of 12 things. A *baker's dozen* contains 12 + 1 = 13 things. The idea of a *baker's dozen* comes from the time in earlier centuries when people always bought their bread rolls at small bakeries. The baker would be afraid that his customers might accuse him of cheating them if he put less than a dozen rolls in their bag. So he always added an extra roll to the dozen, just in case he had miscounted the rolls.

See *dozen*

balance scale A *balance scale* is a scale for measuring masses that consists of two dishes or pans. The dishes hang from a horizontal bar on a pivot. The mass of an item is measured by placing metal weights of known masses in one pan, and the item in the other pan. Metal weights are added to the pan until the two pans balance. The mass of the item is then the same as the total mass of the metal weights.

bank A *bank* is a business that offers financial (money) services to customers. At a *bank* you can deposit your money for safekeeping, borrow money, or move money from your bank account to another account. The *bank* charges you a fee for all these services. You can also earn money (called interest) at the *bank* if you keep your savings there.

See *bank account; deposit; interest*

bank account If you keep your money at a bank you are given your own *bank account* there. Each *bank account* has its own account number. You can add money to your account or withdraw (take out) money from the account.
- Mzi has a savings account at ABSA Bank. Every month his employer pays his salary into his *bank account*. Mzi takes money out of the *bank account* to pay for things he needs. He leaves the rest of the money in the *bank account* until he needs it.

See *bank statement*

bank balance The balance of a bank account is the total amount of money in the account.
- Mzi checks his *bank balance* every month to make sure that his employer has paid his salary into the account.

See *bank account*

bank note A *bank note* is the term sometimes used for paper money (such as R10, R20, R50, R100 and R200 notes).

See *money*

bank statement If you have a bank account, the bank will send you a *bank statement* every month that shows how much money is in your account (the account balance), and lists all the deposits and withdrawals from your account.

STANDARD BANK					
Cape Town		Reg No	1962/00073/06		
PO Box 893, Cape Town , 8000		VAT Reg No	4100105461		
		Customer Care Centre	0860101341		
		23 November 2020			
		204798560			
Mr AB Masongo					
15 Main Rd					
Gardens					
8001					

BANK STATEMENT/TAX INVOICE

ACHIEVER CURRENT ACCOUNT   Account Number 07 389 4261

Month-end Balance   R394,50–

Details	Service fee	Debits	Credits	Date	Balance
Balance brought forward					2 353,95
1B Payment to SOS Vill	3,39	70,00–		10 27	2 283,95
Credit Transfer 9998 2154901999 CT University Pr			10 680,00	11 01	12 963,95
Insurance premium LL 9058	11,69	800,00–		11 05	12 163,95
Autobank Cash Withdrawal GC 12h29	20,00	2 000,00–		11 06	10 163,95
1B Transfer to 07-310-962-0	3,00	8 000,00–		11 10	2 163,95
Closing Balance					R2 163,95

See *bank account; deposit; withdraw*

bar graph/bar chart   A *bar graph* or *bar chart* shows information about amounts of different things. The more things there are, the longer the bar is. A *bar graph* allows you to compare the different amounts of things easily, by comparing the lengths of the bars. The bars can be horizontal or vertical.

- This *bar graph* shows how many learners play each kind of sport.

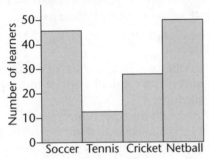

See *block graph; chart; graph*

barter   *Barter* is a form of trade in which people exchange one kind of goods for another, without paying money.

- Susanne *bartered* her fishing rod plus five reels of fishing line for Naledi's bicycle.

base   The *base* of a shape or object is its bottom part.

- The *base* of the bed
- The *base* of the triangle
- The *base* of the cube

See *cube; triangle*

baseline   The *baseline* of an area is a measured line from which triangulations are calculated.

See *triangulation*

base of a number   The *base of a number* is the grouping that we use to count with. In our number system we count in groups of 10. Our number system is a *base 10* number system. Some number systems use other bases, such as *base 2*, which is used by computers (1, 0).

- In the *base 10* number system we group numbers in tens, like this:
  units = single numbers 1–9

tens = 10 × units
hundreds = 10 × tens
thousands = 10 × hundreds
ten thousands = 10 × thousands
hundred thousands = 10 × ten thousands
millions = 10 × hundred thousands

- We write numbers using this base 10 system:
  55 = 5 tens + 5 units
  462 = 4 hundreds + 6 tens + 2 units
  12 036 = 1 ten thousand + 2 thousands
  + no hundreds + 3 tens
  + 6 units

See *binary numbers; duodecimal numbers*

basis   The *basis* of a belief or theory is the set of ideas or facts that people use to support what they believe to be true.

- The *basis* of most religions is a belief in the existence of a divine power.
- The *basis* of our democracy is the belief that all people have equal rights and responsibilities as citizens of South Africa.

bathroom scale   A *bathroom scale* is a scale used at home to measure the mass of a person. It is called a *'bathroom'* scale because many people keep this kind of scale in their bathroom.

bearing   A *bearing* is a way of describing the position of one object in relation to another object. *Bearings* use the north point of the compass, and are measured in degrees. They are always written with three digits.

- To find the *bearing* of the ship at B from a point at A, imagine that you are standing at A and facing north. Rotate (turn) clockwise until you are looking at the ship at B. The angle through which you have rotated is the *bearing* of B from A.

See *angle; degree; digit*

before   *Before* means in front of something (position), or ahead of something in time.

- Khwezi is standing *before* Jonas in the queue.
- *Before* Pumezo goes to school in the morning, he eats his breakfast and brushes his teeth.

See *after*

before noon   The period of time between midnight and midday (noon) can be described as *before noon*.

See *afternoon; a.m.; p.m.*

beginning   The *beginning* of something is the place where it first starts, or the time when it first starts to happen.

- We don't like to miss the *beginning* of the soccer match so we always switch on the TV before the game begins.
- The Nile River is the longest river in the world. Its *beginning* is in Lake Tana, Ethiopia, and it ends in Egypt.

behind   *Behind* means at the back of something, or hidden by it.

- Leila is standing *behind* the door.

See *front*

below   To be *below* something means to be lower (further down) than it.

- The teapot is *below* the glasses on the shelf.

- A submarine sinks *below* the surface of the water.

See *above*

between   1. A thing is *between* two other things if it is in the space that separates the other things.
2. To share something *between* people means to divide it up so that each person gets a share.

- On the number line, 5 is *between* 4 and 6.

- The children shared the packet of crisps *between* themselves.

big   A thing is *big* if it is large in size.
- Jonathan's feet are too *big* to fit into his old soccer boots.

See *small*

bigger than   If we compare a big thing and a small thing, we say that the big thing is *bigger than* the small thing.

- A house is *bigger than* a car.
- 555 is *bigger than* 55.
- −1 is *bigger than* −10
- $\frac{1}{10}$ is *bigger than* $\frac{1}{100}$

See *smaller than*

bilateral symmetry   When a shape has only one line of symmetry, we say it has *bilateral symmetry*. This means that there is only one way to draw a line through the shape, so that the part on one side of the line can fit exactly on top of the part on the other side of the line. (*bi-* means 'two' and *lateral* means 'side'.)

- An apple has *bilateral symmetry*. There is only one line of symmetry for its shape.

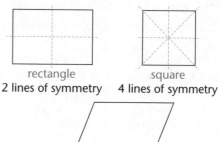

rectangle
2 lines of symmetry

square
4 lines of symmetry

parallelogram
no lines of symmetry

See *line of symmetry; symmetry*

billion   A *billion* is one thousand million or 10^9.
- We write one *billion* as 1 with nine zeroes after it: 1 000 000 000.

binary digit   A *binary digit* is a digit that belongs to a binary system.
- 0 and 1 are *binary digits*.

See *binary system; digit*

binary numbers   The word 'binary' means 'made up of two'. *Binary numbers* are numbers in base 2. They are written with two digits, 0 and 1. In the base 2 system, groupings of units (1s) and twos (multiples of 2) are used:
units, twos, fours, eights, and so on.
- The *binary number* 1101_2 stands for 1 eight, 1 four, 0 twos and 1 unit:

eights	fours	twos	units
1	1	0	1

- In the base 10 number system this equals: $(1 \times 8) + (1 \times 4) + (0 \times 2) + 1 = 13$.
- Computers use *binary numbers*. In an electrical circuit, numbers can symbolise a current flowing (1) or not flowing (0). The number codes used in computer programs are made up of long strings of 0 and 1 combinations that give different instructions to the computer's electrical circuits.

See *base of a number; binary system*

binary system   A *binary system* is a number system using base 2 numbers. In a *binary system* the numbers are expressed using only the two binary digits 0 and 1.

See *base of a number; binary numbers*

binomial expression   A *binomial expression* is an expression consisting of two terms connected by a plus (+) or minus (–) sign.
- These are examples of *binomial expressions*:

  $x - y$

  $78a^2 + 3$

See *expression; term*

bisect   To *bisect* means to divide something into two equal parts.
- The line EF *bisects* the rectangle ABCD. The two smaller rectangles ABFE and EFCD are exactly the same size.

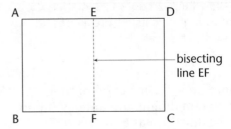

See *rectangle*

bisector   A *bisector* is a line that divides a shape into two equal parts.
- Angle AOB is divided into two equal angles by the *bisector* OD.

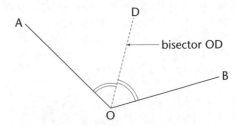

See *angle; angle bisector; bisect*

block   1. A *block* is a solid piece of stone or wood.
2. A *block* in a diagram is a square or rectangle. It is sometimes part of a grid of *blocks* in the diagram.

Which province do you live in? Tick the correct block:	
☐ WC	☐ Gau
☐ NC	☐ Lim
☐ EC	☐ KZN
☐ FS	☐ NW
☐ MP	

See *block diagram; block graph*

block diagram   A *block diagram* is a plan drawn in outline to show the workings or form of something using blocks.

See *block; diagram*

block graph   A *block graph* is a graph that uses bars to show and compare the amounts of different groups of things. It can also be called a bar graph or bar chart.

See *bar graph*

BODMAS *BODMAS* is the abbreviation for a rule that we use in arithmetic, when we combine different operations in one calculation. The rule states that we should do the operations in this order:
Brackets
Of (change 'of' to × and multiply)
Divide
Multiply
Add
Subtract
See *arithmetic; operation*

border The *border* of a thing is its edge, rim or margin.
• There is a lace *border* around the bottom of the skirt.
• The *border* of Namibia meets South Africa in the Northern Cape.

bottom The *bottom* of something can be:
1. its lowest point in space
2. its position underneath everything else
3. the underside of that thing.
• In some places the *bottom* of the sea is 3 km below the level of the water surface.
• The tennis ball was right at the *bottom* of the basket.
• Stephen wrote his name on the *bottom* of the box.

See *top*

brackets *Brackets* show which numbers in a calculation are combined together. There are three types of brackets:
• round *brackets*: ( )
• curly *brackets*: { }
• square *brackets*: [ ]
Round brackets are used in arithmetic calculations. Curly brackets are used to group the numbers in a set. Square brackets are not often used.
• $3(x + 2y) + 2x(x + y)$
• The set of even numbers from 2 to 10
  E = {2, 4, 6, 8, 10}

See *arithmetic; set*

breadth The *breadth* of a shape is the measurement of its shorter side. Another word for *breadth* is width.
• The *breadth* of this rectangle is 4 cm. The length is 6 cm.

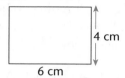

See *length; width*

break up To *break up* a number means to separate it into its smaller parts.
• We can *break up* the number 20 in many ways. For example:
20 = 10 + 10
20 = 5 + 6 + 9
20 = 1 + 1 + 1 + 1 + 1 + 1 + 1 + 1 + 1 + 1 + 1 + 1 + 1 + 1 + 1 + 1 + 1 + 1 + 1 + 1

broad A thing is *broad* if its breadth (its measurement from side to side) is large. Another word for *broad* is wide.
• The river is narrow in many places but near the village it is very *broad*.

See *narrow*

broken-line graph A *broken-line graph* is a graph that uses short line segments to show number information. It is different from a continuous line graph where one continuous line shows the number information.

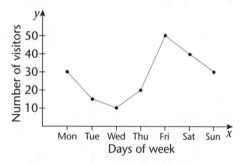

See *continuous graph; line segment*

budget A *budget* is a plan that shows how you intend to spend and make money. In the *budget*, you list each thing you will pay for, with its cost (expenses). You also list all the money you will make (income). The *budget* lets you see whether you will make enough money to pay for all the things you have listed. *To budget* means to prepare a *budget* so that you know whether you have enough money to buy what you want or need.

See *income*

button (calculator) The *buttons* on a calculator are the small knobs marked with numbers or mathematical signs. You press a *button* to enter a number or operation into the calculator.

See *calculator; calculator key*

buy To *buy* something means to give money in exchange for a thing that you want or need.
- Refilwe is saving money so that she can *buy* a new car.

See *barter; purchase; sell*

C

calculate To *calculate* something means to find the answer to a question using mathematical methods such as arithmetic or algebra. The question and the answer usually contain number quantities.
- Question: *Calculate* the value of
$$35 + \frac{1}{2} - 25,5$$
  Answer:　$35 + \frac{1}{2} - 25,5 = 35 + 0,5 - 25,5$
$$= 35,5 - 25,5$$
$$= 10$$

See *algebra; arithmetic; calculation*

calculate mentally You *calculate mentally* if you do a calculation in your head, without writing down the parts of the calculation as you work it out.

See *calculate*

calculation A *calculation* is a mathematical problem that you solve to get a particular value.
- Astronomers do many *calculations* to find out the exact distances to different planets and stars.

See *calculate*

calculation rule A *calculation rule* is a method of doing a calculation that must always follow the same set of steps (or a rule) to get the answer.
- In a calculation with more than one arithmetic operation (addition, subtraction, multiplication, division), you must always use the BODMAS *calculation rule*.

See *BODMAS*

calculator A *calculator* is a machine that does mathematical calculations very quickly.

See *calculator key*

calculator key, keypad The buttons on a calculator are called keys. You press the keys to give instructions to the calculator. The front section of the calculator with all the *calculator keys* is called the *keypad*.

See *button (calculator)*; *calculator*

calendar A *calendar* shows the days and months of the year.
- The *calendar* for 2006 shows that 16 June fell on a Friday.

See *month*

calendar month The calendar that we use to record and calculate time uses years, divided into months. One year is divided into 12 months from January to December. These are called *calendar months*. Some societies use months measured according to the moon. These are called 'lunar months'.
- The second *calendar month* of the year is February.

cancel We *cancel* a fraction when we divide the numerator and denominator of the fraction by the same number. We do this to simplify the fraction (write it in smaller numbers).
- To *cancel* the fraction $\frac{25}{40}$ we divide the numerator and the denominator by 5:
$$\frac{^5 25}{40_8} = \frac{5}{8}$$

See *denominator*; *fraction*; *numerator*; *simplify*

capacity The *capacity* of a container is the amount of liquid that it can hold.
- The *capacity* of this milk bottle is 1 litre.

See *metric system*; *volume*

cardinal number The *cardinal number* of a set is the number of elements in the set.
- The *cardinal number* of the set B = {7, 14, 21, 28} is 4, because there are four elements in the set.

See *element of a set*; *set*

Cartesian plane The *Cartesian plane*, named after the mathematician René Descartes, is the plane that is formed by a vertical number line (*y*-axis) and a horizontal number line (*x*-axis) intersecting at 0. Points on this plane are described using an *x*-value and a *y*-value. These points are called coordinates.

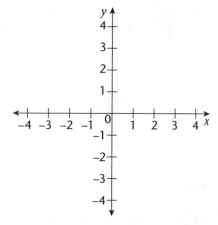

See *coordinates*; *horizontal*; *plane*; *vertical*

Celsius We use units called degrees *Celsius* to measure the temperature of something (how hot or cold it is). The man who developed these measuring units was a Swedish astronomer called Anders Celsius – the units are named after him. There are other measuring systems for temperature that use different units, such as Fahrenheit and Kelvin.
The measuring unit is written as °C.
- The temperature at midday today was 21 °C. Tonight it will go down to 7 °C.

See *Fahrenheit*; *thermometer*

cent A *cent* is one hundredth of a rand.
- I have 99 *cents* – almost R1!

centimetre   A *centimetre* is a unit for measuring length. There are 100 *centimetres* in one metre.

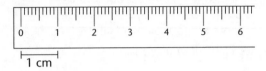

1 cm

See *length; SI units*

centre of a circle   The *centre of a circle* is a point in the circle that is the same distance from all the points on the edge (circumference) of the circle.

- Point O is at the *centre of this circle*. The distance from any point on the edge of the circle to O (the radius) is the same as the distance from any other point on the edge to O.

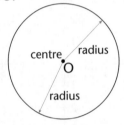

See *circle; midpoint; radius*

century   A *century* is a time period of 100 years.

- The 20th *century* started on 1 January 1901 and ended on 31 December 2000.
- Jeanne was 122 years old when she died. She was more than a *century* old.

See *millennium*

change (money)   If you give a salesperson more money for something than it costs, the salesperson will give you back the extra money. This is called *change*.

- I bought a book for R85. I gave the salesperson a R100 note and she gave me back R15 in *change*.

See *money*

chart   A *chart* is an information sheet that shows tables, graphs or other number facts.

- This *chart* shows what the healthy mass is for people of different heights.

Height range (without shoes) in metres	Age in years							
	10	11	12	13	14	15	16	17–18
	Mass in kilograms							
1.19–1.21	22–24							
1.22–1.24	23–25	23–26						
1.25–1.27	24–26	24–26						
1.27–1.29	25–27	25–27	26–28					
1.30–1.31	26–28	27–29	27–29					
1.32–1.34	27–30	28–30	28–31					
1.35–1.36	29–31	29–31	30–32	30–32				
1.37–1.39	30–32	30–32	31–33	31–34				
1.40–1.41	32–34	32–35	33–35	33–36	34–36			
1.42–1.44	34–36	35–37	35–38	36–39	36–40			
1.45–1.46	36–37	36–38	37–39	38–41	38–41	39–43		
1.47–1.49	37–39	38–40	38–40	40–42	41–43	42–46	43–49	
1.50–1.51	39–41	40–41	40–42	42–44	43–45	44–47	45–50	46–52
1.52–1.54	41–43	42–44	44–46	45–47	46–49	46–51	48–53	48–53
1.55–1.56	42–44	43–45	44–66	46–48	46–49	47–51	48–53	49–55
1.57–1.59	44–46	45–47	46–47	47–50	48–51	49–53	50–55	51–56
1.60–1.62	46–47	46–48	47–49	49–51	51–54	51–55	52–56	54–59
1.63–1.64	46–49	47–50	49–51	51–53	52–55	53–56	54–58	56–61
1.65–1.67	48–50	49–51	51–53	52–55	53–57	54–58	56–59	58–62
1.68–1.69		51–53	53–55	54–57	55–59	56–60	57–61	60–64
1.70–1.72		52–55	54–56	55–59	57–61	58–61	59–62	61–66
1.73–1.74			56–58	56–61	59–62	60–63	61–64	63–68
1.75–1.77			57–60	58–62	61–64	62–65	63–66	63–68
1.78–1.79				59–64	62–66	64–68	64–71	65–73
1.80–1.82				61–66	64–68	66–71	66–73	66–76
1.83–1.84					66–70	67–71	68–74	68–77
1.85–1.87					68–71	67–74	70–76	70–80
1.88–1.90						71–75	72–77	72–77

See *graph; table (data)*

check   To *check* something means to test whether it is true.

- After you do an arithmetic calculation in your head, you can *check* your answer by doing the same calculation on a calculator.

check digit   A *check digit* is a digit that is added to numbers to test their accuracy and to check that the digits have been correctly recorded.

See *data; digit*

cheque   A *cheque* is a bank form that you can use to move money from your bank account to another person's bank account, without using cash (money notes and coins). Banks give their customers cheque books to use; each cheque book contains 20 *cheque* forms, printed with the customer's name and account number.

• Thuli sent her mother a *cheque* for R250 as a birthday present. Her mother took the *cheque* to the bank and exchanged it for cash.

See *bank account*

choose   To *choose* means to pick out (select) one or more things from a group of things.

• You can't have all the sweets! *Choose* the one sweet that you really want.

chord   A *chord* is a line inside a circle that joins two points on the circumference (edge) of the circle. If the *chord* passes through the midpoint of the circle it is called the diameter of the circle.

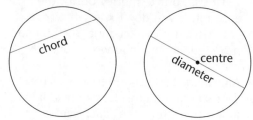

See *circle; circumference; midpoint*

circle   A *circle* is a round two-dimensional shape in which all the points on the edge of the shape are the same distance from the centre.

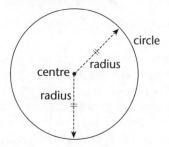

See *circumference; radius*

circle graph   A *circle graph* is a graph that is shaped like a circle.

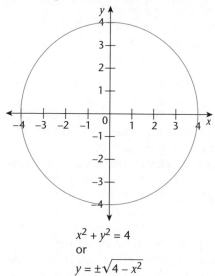

$$x^2 + y^2 = 4$$
or
$$y = \pm\sqrt{4 - x^2}$$

See *circle; graph*

circular   An object is *circular* if it has the shape of a circle.

• A plate is *circular*.

See *circle*

circumcircle   The *circumcircle*, or circumscribed circle, of a triangle is a circle that passes through all three vertices of the triangle. The centre of this *circumcircle* is the point where the three perpendicular bisectors of the triangle intersect.

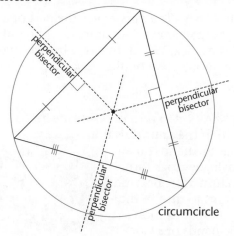

See *perpendicular bisector; triangle; vertex*

circumference   The *circumference* of a circle is the distance all around the edge of the circle. It is the perimeter length (edge) of the circle.

See *circle; perimeter*

circumference

classify   To *classify* a group of things means to arrange them into different types or categories of things.
- Scientists *classify* animals into different groups such as insects, fish, mammals, reptiles, and so on.

class intervals   When statistical data are being collected, they are sometimes grouped together and recorded in *class intervals* that group sub-sections of the data.
- Exam marks can be grouped in *class intervals* like this:

Mark	Tally	Frequency
40–49	//	2
50–59	///	3
60–69	*LHT* /	6

See *data*

clock   A *clock* is a machine for measuring time.

See *analogue clock; clock face; digital clock*

clock face   The *clock face* is the part of a clock that shows the numbers and hands of the clock. We tell the time by reading the information on the *clock face*.

See *clock*

clockwise   To turn *clockwise* means to turn in the same direction that the hands on an analogue clock turn. To turn anticlockwise means to turn in the opposite direction to the hands of a clock.

See *analogue clock; anticlockwise*

closed   To *close* an object means to make all its edges touch so that there is no opening into the shape. When you do this you have a *closed* shape.
- This is a *closed* cube. It has no opening on any side or edge.

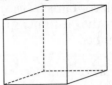

See *cube*

clue   A *clue* is a piece of information that you can use to help you solve a problem or answer a question.
- Can you guess what is in the basket? Here's a *clue*: it makes the sound 'meow'.

code   A *code* is a group of letters and/or numbers that is used to keep some information safe and secret.
- Each person with a bank account has a PIN *code* – a secret number that they must use to take money out of the account. If you don't know the *code*, you can't use the account. You should never tell anyone else what your PIN *code* is.
- A message can be written in a secret *code* so that no one else can read it unless they know the *code*. Here is message in Morse *code*:

—	•	•—	—•—•	••••	•	•—•

To find out what the message is, use the Morse *code* alphabet table on page 149 of this dictionary.

See *bank account*

coefficient   The *coefficient* of a symbol in an algebraic expression is the number that the symbol is multiplied by.
- In the algebraic expression $3x + 11x^2 + 2y$, the *coefficient* of x is 3, the *coefficient* of x^2 is 11, and the *coefficient* of y is 2.

See *algebra; expression*

coin   A *coin* is a piece of metal that we use as money. It has two sides: heads and tails. The money value is stamped on one side of the *coin*.

co-interior angles   *Co-interior angles* are formed when a transversal crosses two lines. The two angles formed in this way on the same side of the transversal and between the parallel lines are co-interior. If the two lines crossed by the transversal are parallel, then the *co-interior angles* are supplementary.

See *alternate angles; parallel; supplementary angles; transversal*

collect   To *collect* things means to find or fetch them and bring them together.
• For a science project, Darryl *collected* ten different types of flowers from his garden and brought them to class.

collinear points   Points that lie on the same straight line are called *collinear points*.
• In this diagram, the points A, C and B are *collinear*, the points E, C, F, and D are *collinear*, but the points A, C and E are not *collinear*.

colour   *Colour* is how our eyes see different wavelengths of light. The shortest wavelength of light is violet. The longest wavelength of light is red. When light hits our eyes we see all the different *colours* of the wavelengths of light rays.
• The rainbow has seven *colours*: red, orange, yellow, green, blue, indigo, violet. These *colours* come from the different wavelengths in the sunlight that passes through raindrops.

column   A *column* is a vertical arrangement of numbers, words or shapes (from top to bottom on the page)
• There are four *columns* in this table.

Column 1	Column 2	Column 3	Column 4

See *row; table; vertical*

combine, combination   To *combine* things means to bring separate things together into one group. This group is called the *combination* of the separate things.
• If you *combine* the numbers in set A with the numbers in set B, you get set C:
  ‣ A = {1, 3, 5, 7, 9}
    B = {2, 4, 6, 8, 10}
    C = {1, 2, 3, 4, 5, 6, 7, 8, 9, 10}
  ‣ A = {100, 103, 105, 106}
    B = {101, 103, 105}
    C = {100, 101, 103, 105, 106}

comma   A *comma* is a punctuation mark. You use it in sentences to separate things in a list, or to show where there is a short pause. The decimal *comma* is the symbol that separates whole numbers from the decimal fractions in a decimal number.
• Keith bought a dictionary, a note book, a calculator, a ruler and three pens.
• The decimal *comma* comes between the units and the tenths in these decimal fractions:
12,3
1,345
100,006

See *decimal fraction*

commission   *Commission* is a kind of payment that salespeople earn. For every item that they sell, they get paid a percentage of the price of the item. This percentage is called the *commission*.
• Zola earns 10% *commission* on all the school books that he sells. This month he sold books worth R5 000. His *commission* is 10% of R5 000, which is R500.

See *percentage*

common denominator   To add fractions, their denominators need to be the same. A *common denominator* is a multiple of the denominators of all the fractions to be added. Once the fractions all have this *common denominator*, you can add their numerators together.

- Add $\frac{3}{4} + \frac{1}{5}$.
  First find a *common denominator* for the two fractions by comparing their multiples:
  multiples of 4: 4, 8, 12, 16, 20, 24, ...
  multiples of 5: 5, 10, 15, 20, 25, ...
  So 20 is a *common denominator* for these two fractions.
  $4 \times 5 = 20$ and $5 \times 4 = 20$.
  Now re-write the fractions with this common denominator:
  $$\frac{3}{4} = \frac{3 \times 5}{4 \times 5} = \frac{15}{20}$$
  $$\frac{1}{5} = \frac{1 \times 4}{5 \times 4} = \frac{4}{20}$$
  Then $\frac{3}{4} + \frac{1}{5} = \frac{15}{20} + \frac{4}{20} = \frac{19}{20}$.

See *denominator; numerator*

common elements   1. To have something 'in common' with another person means to have the same thing as that person.
2. *Common elements* are elements that occur in two or more sets that you are comparing.

- If we compare the set
  $Y = \{1, 2, 3, 4, 5, 6, 7, 8, 9, 10, 11, 12\}$
  and the set
  $Z = \{3, 4, 5, 11, 12, 13, 15, 18, 21\}$
  we see that the *common elements* of the two sets are 3, 4, 5, 11 and 12.

See *element of a set*

common factor   The factors of a number are the numbers that divide into it exactly. If two different numbers have some factors that are the same, these are called *common factors*.

- Factors of 20: 1, 2, 4, 5, 10, 20
  Factors of 30: 1, 2, 3, 5, 6, 10, 15, 30
  Therefore the *common factors* of 20 and 30 are 1, 2, 5 and 10.

See *factor*

common fraction   A *common fraction* is a fraction written in the form $\frac{a}{b}$ where a (the numerator) and b (the denominator) are integers and $b \neq 0$. A decimal fraction is not a common fraction because it is written using decimal places, not numerators and denominators.

- $\frac{3}{4}$ is a *common fraction*, whereas 0,75 is a decimal fraction.

See *denominator; integer; numerator*

common multiple   If two numbers have some multiples that are the same, these are called *common multiples* of the two numbers.

- Multiples of 3: 3, 6, 9, 12, 15, 18, 21, 24, 27, 30, 33, 36, ...
  Multiples of 4: 4, 8, 12, 16, 20, 24, 28, 32, 36, 40, 44, ...
  Therefore 12, 24, 36 are *common multiples* of 3 and 4. (Note that there will be more *common multiples* of 3 and 4 if you write down more multiples of each number.)

See *multiple*

commutative   Some arithmetic operations are *commutative*: this means that you can write the numbers in the operation in any order. Addition and multiplication are *commutative*. Subtraction and division are not *commutative*.

- Addition is *commutative*:
  $3 + 4 = 7$ and $4 + 3 = 7$
- Multiplication is *commutative*:
  $3 \times 4 = 12$ and $4 \times 3 = 12$
- Subtraction is not *commutative*:
  $3 - 4 = -1$ but $4 - 3 = 1$
- Division is not *commutative*:
  $3 \div 4 = \frac{3}{4}$ but $4 \div 3 = \frac{4}{3} = 1\frac{1}{3}$

See *arithmetic; operation*

compare   To *compare* two or more things means to look for the ways in which they are the same and the ways in which they are different.

- If we *compare* a square and a rectangle we see that they have the following in common (the same):

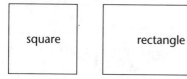

- They both have 4 sides.
- They both have 4 corners that are right angles.
- They are different in the following ways:
  - The square has 4 sides that are all the same length.
  - The rectangle has 2 opposite sides that are shorter than the other 2 opposite sides.

See *comparison*

comparison   A *comparison* is the act of comparing two or more things.
- If you make a *comparison* between a square shape and a rectangular shape, you will see that they are the same in some ways but different in other ways.

See *compare*

compass (geometric)   See *pair of compasses*

compass (magnetic), compass points
A *magnetic compass* is an instrument for finding direction. It has a magnetic needle that always points to the North Pole. The directions north, south, east and west are marked on the face of the compass. These are called the cardinal (main) *compass points*.

See *direction; points of the compass*

complementary angles   *Complementary angles* are angles that add up to 90°.
- In this diagram the two angles ABC and CBD are *complementary angles* because 28° + 62° = 90°. Angle ABC is the complement of angle CBD; angle CBD is the complement of angle ABC.

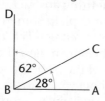

See *angle*

complete (adjective)   A thing is *complete* if it has all its parts and nothing is missing.
- The jigsaw puzzle is *complete* – there are no puzzle pieces missing.

complete (verb)   To *complete* something means to finish making it, or to add all the parts so that it is a whole thing.
- The builders must *complete* the house before winter comes. They must still put on the roof and put in a door.
- *Complete* this statement:
  350 + _____ = 425
  To *complete* the statement you must fill in the missing number values:
  350 + <u>75</u> = 425

complete circle   A *complete circle* is a full circle with no gaps in the circumference.

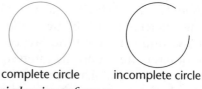

complete circle   incomplete circle

See *circle; circumference*

complex calculation   A *complex calculation* is a calculation that has different parts. You need to do each separate part of the calculation to find the answer.
- 1 250 + (36 × 57) × (5 000 ÷ 0,75) – 89 is a *complex calculation* – you need to do the parts of the calculation one by one to find the answer.

See *calculation*

composite number   A *composite number* is a whole number made up (composed) of two other whole numbers multiplied together, as long as neither of these numbers is 1.
- 12 is a *composite number* because it can be composed by multiplying 3 × 4, or 2 × 6.
- 11 is not a *composite number* because it can only be composed by multiplying 11 × 1. There are no other whole numbers that you can multiply together to get 11. Numbers that are not composite are called prime numbers.

See *prime number; whole number*

compound events   *Compound events* are two or more statistical events that are analysed together to find outcomes and probabilities.
• An example of a *compound event* is to toss three coins at the same time.

See *event; outcome; probability*

compound interest   *Compound interest* is a type of interest that your money can earn if you leave it in a bank account instead of spending it. You may also pay *compound interest* if you borrow money from the bank or from a loan agent. *Compound interest* is calculated by adding a percentage of the money to the first amount that is in the account, after a certain time (such as a month or a year). Then this new amount earns more *compound interest*, which is calculated by adding a percentage of the new amount after a second period of time. So you earn (or pay) interest on the interest, as well as on the original amount of money. The total amount of money therefore grows faster than if the money were earning simple interest.
• Zithulele has R100 in a bank savings account. The bank pays 7% per year *compound interest* on savings. After one year Zithulele has:
R100 + (7% of R100) = R100 + R7
= R107 in his savings account.
After two years he has:
R107 + (7% of R107) = R107 + R7,49
= R114,49 in his account.
After three years he has:
R114,49 + (7% of R114,49)
= R114,49 + R8,01
= R122,50 in his account.
Zithulele is earning 7% interest on his R100 and also 7% interest on the extra interest amount that gets added every year.

See *interest; simple interest*

compound measure   A *compound measure* is a measure of something that is made up of two (or more) separate measurements.

• Speed is a *compound measure*: it is made up of the measurement of distance and the measurement of time. If a car travels at 60 km/h, we know this because we measured how far the car went (60 km) in a certain length of time (1 h).

See *measurement; speed*

concave   A *concave* shape curves inwards like a bowl.

See *convex*

concave polygon   A *concave polygon* is a polygon in which some sides point 'inwards'. In a *concave polygon* one of the interior angles is a reflex angle (between 180° and 360°).
• These are examples of *concave polygons*:

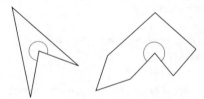

See *concave; convex polygon; polygon*

concentric   Two or more circles are *concentric* if they have the same centre (midpoint).

centre

See *centre of a circle; circle*

concept   A *concept* is a general thought or idea, something abstract, that we use to describe or explain something.
• Scientists use *concepts* like 'gravity' and 'mass' to help them describe the properties of the planets and stars.
• In high school you learn about the *concept* of similarity in geometry.

concurrent Two or more lines that all pass through the same point are *concurrent*.

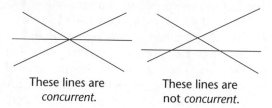

These lines are *concurrent*.   These lines are not *concurrent*.

See *line*

cone A *cone* is a three-dimensional shape with a circular base that tapers (narrows) to a point. The point is called the vertex of the *cone*.

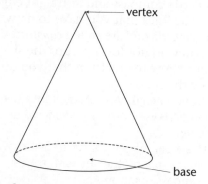

vertex

base

See *three-dimensional*

congruent Two (or more) shapes or objects are *congruent* if they are exactly the same shape and size. If two shapes are *congruent* then they can be moved so that one shape fits exactly on top of the other shape.

- These two rectangles are *congruent*:

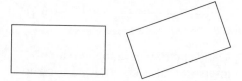

- These two rectangles are not *congruent*:

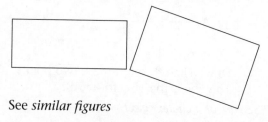

See *similar figures*

congruent angles Angles that have the same size (degrees) are *congruent angles*.

145°   145°

congruent triangles Two triangles are *congruent triangles* if the angles and side lengths are the same in both triangles.

- These two triangles are *congruent*.

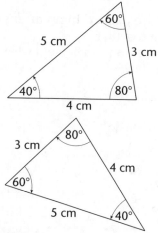

See *triangle*

conical An object is *conical* if it has the shape of a cone.

See *cone*

conic section A *conic section* is a curve that occurs when a plane intersects (cuts through) a cone. The *conic sections* will have different shapes, depending on the angle at which they intersect the cone.

- An ellipse, a parabola and a hyperbola are examples of *conic sections*:

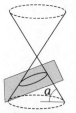  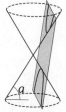

An **ellipse:** The angle of slope of the plane is less than angle *a*.

A **parabola:** The angle of slope of the plane is equal to angle *a*.

A **hyperbola:** The angle of slope of the plane is greater than angle *a*.

See *cone; curve; plane*

conjecture A *conjecture* is a statement that a mathematician could make after noticing a pattern in a small group of data, and hoping the pattern will occur in all cases of the data. Once the mathematician has made the *conjecture*, the next step is to find a proof that the statement is true in all cases.

See *data*

connect To *connect* things means to join them together.

- *Connect* the dots to find out what the picture shows.

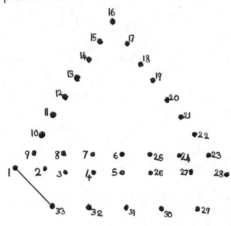

- *Connect* the points to draw the graph.

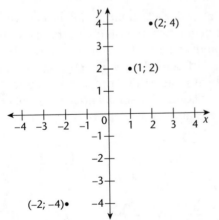

consecutive *Consecutive* numbers are numbers that directly follow each other in a sequence. 1, 2, 3, 4 are *consecutive* whole numbers.

See *counting numbers*

constant, constant term A *constant* is a quantity in an equation or expression that does not change, even if other parts of the equation or expression change.

- In the algebraic expression $3a^2 + 16a + 45$, the values of the first two terms, $3a^2$ and $16a$, will change depending on the number value that you choose for a. But the value of the third term, 45, does not change because it is a number value. 45 is the *constant term* in this expression.

See *equation; expression; term*

construction A *construction* is a method for making accurate geometrical drawings of shapes. *Constructions* can be made using a geometric compass and a straight edge (a ruler). The lines that you have to draw to do the *construction* are called *construction lines*. They do not form part of the shape but they show the method that you used to draw the shape.

- To bisect the line AB (divide it into two equal parts) using *construction*, we do the following:
  - Use a pair of compasses to first draw a circular arc on the line with the compass point on A.

  - Then draw another circular arc on the line with the compass point on B without adjusting the pair of compasses.

  - Mark a point where the two arcs intersect (cut each other) above and below line AB.

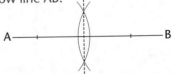

  - Draw a line through these two points. This line is the bisector of AB.

See *arc of a circle; bisect*

contain   To *contain* something means to enclose it or to include it.

- The box *contains* all Dora's sports equipment.

container   A *container* is any three-dimensional object that is used to contain something.

contents   *Contents* is a general word that describes 'everything that is in a container'.

See *container*

continue   To *continue* means to carry on doing something or to keep moving in the same direction, without changing anything.

- The hospital is about 3 km from here. Just *continue* on this road until you see it.
- Once you've learnt how to swim, it's important to *continue* practising every day so that your muscles don't lose their strength.

continuous graph   A graph is a *continuous graph* if it can be drawn without lifting the pencil off the paper.

- A straight-line graph is a *continuous graph*. Every point on the straight line represents a particular value of the graph in terms of x and y.

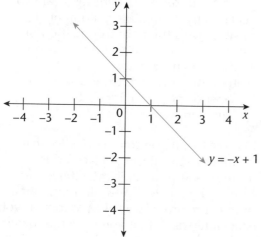

$y = -x + 1$

See *graph*

continuous variable   A *continuous variable* is a variable that can take any value in a given interval.

- The height of an adult person is a *continuous variable* (usually in the interval from 150 cm to 200 cm).

See *interval; variable*

converge   1. Two or more lines *converge* if they all move in the direction of the same point.
2. When the terms of a sequence get closer and closer to a number L so that the differences between them and L approach 0, the sequence is said to *converge* on L. The number L is called the limit of the sequence.

- These three lines all *converge* on the point P.

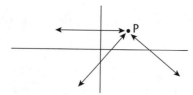

- The sequence $2, 1\frac{1}{2}, 1\frac{1}{4}, 1\frac{1}{8}, 1\frac{1}{16}, \ldots$ *converges* to the limit 1.
  The sequence $\frac{1}{2}, \frac{1}{4}, \frac{1}{8}, \frac{1}{16}, \frac{1}{32}, \ldots$ *converges* to the limit 0.

converse   A statement that is logically opposite to another statement, is the *converse* of that statement.

conversion   A *conversion* happens when one thing changes into another thing, or when one thing changes from one state into another state.

- If you travel outside South Africa, you must organise the *conversion* of your rands into the currency of the country you are going to.
- The *conversion* of ice into water happens when the tempera-ture rises above freezing point.

See *convert*

conversion graph A *conversion graph* is used to convert one set of number values into another set of number values. It is useful when you need to convert measurements from one measuring unit into a different measuring unit.

- This *conversion graph* can be used to convert miles into kilometres.

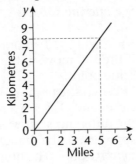

See *graph*

convert To *convert* something means to change it from one form into another form.

- *Convert* these decimal fractions to proper fractions:

$$0,25 = \frac{1}{4}$$

$$0,654 = \frac{654}{1\,000}$$

convex A *convex* shape is a shape that curves outwards, like the surface of a sphere.

- The lens of the eye is *convex*.

See *concave*

convex polygon A polygon is *convex* if all of its edges go 'outwards' rather than 'inwards'.

- These are *convex polygons*:

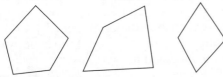

See *concave polygon*

coordinates *Coordinates* in the coordinate system are numbers or letters that describe the position of a point on a graph or chart, or the position of a place on a map. There are two numbers or letters for every coordinate position – it is sometimes called a *coordinate* pair ('pair' means 'two things').

- On a map, the position of every place is described by a number–letter *coordinate* pair. For example, the *coordinates* for Soweto are 26°S 27°E.
- On this graph, the position of any point is given by two *coordinates* – an *x*-value and a *y*-value. The *coordinates* are written as a pair of numbers $(x; y)$. The horizontal (*x*-) *coordinate* is always written first, and the vertical (*y*-) *coordinate* is written second. These are called Cartesian *coordinates*, after the mathematician René Descartes who invented this *coordinate* system for describing position.

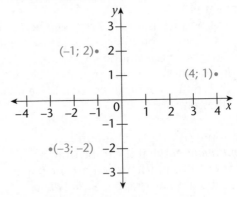

See *Cartesian plane; graph; horizontal; vertical*

correct To *correct* something means to replace any wrong information or answers with the right information or answers. A *correct* answer is an answer that has no mistakes.

- The teacher *corrects* the learner's test paper by placing a tick next to every *correct* answer.

correct to If you round off a decimal number to two decimal places, this rounded-off number is then *correct to* two decimal places. You can round off a number to any place value, as long as you state afterwards that you have rounded it off *correct to* that place value.

- The number 14,376 becomes 14,38 if we round it off *correct to* two decimal places.

See *decimal; decimal places*

correlation   If you have two variables and as one changes the other variable also changes in a related way, then there is a *correlation* between the two variables.

• Tall people usually have longer arm spans than shorter people. There is a *correlation* between a person's height and their arm span.

See *variable*

correspond   Two groups of things *correspond* if the one group matches the other group in some way.

• The number of hats on the hat stand *corresponds* to the number of people in the room.

corresponding angles   *Corresponding angles* are the angles in the same position between any of a group of parallel lines and the transversal line that cuts these parallel lines. These *corresponding angles* are equal.

• In the diagram:
  ‣ angles *a* and *e* are *corresponding angles*,
  ‣ angles *b* and *f* are *corresponding angles*, and so on.

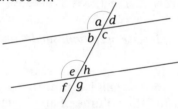

See *parallel; transversal*

corresponding points   In transformations such as enlargements, reflections, rotations and translations, points that map onto each other are called *corresponding points*.

• In this rotation, A and A' are *corresponding points*, and B and B' are *corresponding points*.

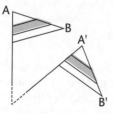

• In this rotation, Q and Q' are *corresponding points*, and P and P' are *corresponding points*.

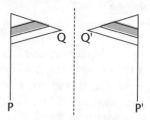

See *enlargement; reflection; rotation; transformation; translation*

cost   The *cost* of something is the amount of money you must pay to have it.

• The *cost* of a holiday in Cape Town is R3 500. This includes the *cost* of the air fare and the *cost* of the hotel accommodation.

cost price   The *cost price* of an item is the amount of money that it costs to produce (make) the item.

• The *cost price* of this car is R45 000. This includes the cost of all the parts, the wages for the factory workers who build the car, and the cost of running the machines in the factory.

See *profit; selling price*

counter   A *counter* is a table in a bank or shop across which the money or goods are passed from the staff to the customer.

counting numbers   The *counting numbers* are all the natural numbers 1, 2, 3, ... This set of numbers is sometimes called the set of whole numbers.

• 11, 200, 520 000, 365 000 000 and 57 are all examples of *counting numbers*. Fractions and decimals are not *counting numbers*. Negative numbers (integers) are not *counting numbers*.

See *consecutive; natural numbers; whole number*

cross out   To *cross out* something means to draw a line through it to show that it must be ignored.

- ~~33 + 44 = 66~~
  33 + 44 = 77

cross-section   A *cross-section* is a slice through a three-dimensional object, usually parallel to its base or end.

- These are examples of *cross-section* slices through different shapes:

See *parallel*

crossword puzzle   A *crossword puzzle* is a word puzzle that uses a grid of squares. You have to fill in the missing letters in the squares to make complete words. The puzzle gives clues to help you work out what the words should be. The words run horizontally and vertically on the grid, and you have to find letters that fit the words in both directions.

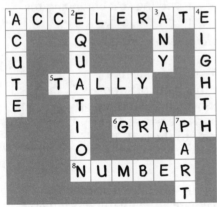

Across
1 To speed up an already moving object.
5 A way of counting items by making a mark for each item, often done in groups of five.
6 A way of showing the relationship between two sets of number values in the form of a picture.
8 A concept for describing how many thing there are.

Down
1 The angle size that is less than 90 degrees.
2 A mathematical statement that uses an = sign to state that one expression is equal to another expression.
3 Does not matter which one you choose from a group of objects.
4 One part of a whole that has been divided into eight parts.
7 A section of something, not the whole thing.

See *horizontal; vertical*

cube   A *cube* is a three-dimensional object. All its faces (sides) are squares and all its edges are the same length. All its corners form right angles (90°).

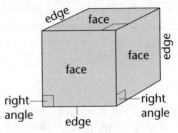

See *cuboid; three-dimensional*

cube of a number (cubed number)   The *cube of a number* is that number to the power of 3; that is, the number multiplied by itself three times.

- The cube of 5 is $5^3 = 5 \times 5 \times 5 = 125$

See *cube root; power of a number*

cube root   The *cube root* is the number that you must multiply by itself three times to get the cube of a number. The symbol for the *cube root* of any number x is $\sqrt[3]{x}$.

- The *cube root* of 125 is 5, because $125 = 5 \times 5 \times 5 = 5^3$.

See *cube; inverse operation; square root*

cubic unit, cubic centimetre, cubic metre   A *cubic unit* is a unit that we use to measure the volume of an object. This corresponds to the three measurements that we multiply together to find volume – length, breadth and height. The *cubic units* that we use most often to measure volume are the *cubic centimetre* and the *cubic metre*.

- The *cubic centimetre* – written as 1 cm^3 – is the volume of a cube that has length = 1 cm, breadth = 1 cm and height = 1 cm. It is also abbreviated as cc, especially when referring to the engine capacity of a car or motorbike.
- The *cubic metre* – written as 1 m^3 – is the volume of a cube that has length = 1 m, breadth = 1 m and height = 1 m.

- The volume of this cuboid is 56 cm³ – it consists of 56 *cubic centimetres*. We can calculate this volume by multiplying the length × breadth × height of the cuboid, in centimetre units:

$l \times b \times h = 7 \times 2 \times 4 = 56$ cm³.

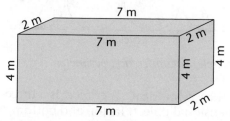

See *measuring unit; volume*

cubit   A *cubit* is a measuring unit for length that was used in some ancient societies. One *cubit* is the length from your elbow to the tip of your middle finger – about 43 to 53 cm.

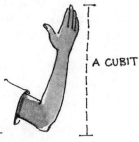

A CUBIT

The word *cubit* comes from the Latin word for 'elbow'.

See *length*

cuboid   A *cuboid* is a rectangular box.
- Many boxes are *cuboid* shapes:

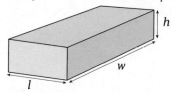

See *cube; edge; face; three-dimensional*

cumulative frequency   *Cumulative frequency* is a way of analysing statistical data. It is calculated by adding up (accumulating) the frequencies of individual data events.
- In this table, the second column shows the number of students who got 0, 1, 2, …, 10 marks in a test. The third

column shows *cumulative frequency*, by adding up the frequencies in the second column. So, for example, 26 students had a mark of 7 or less. 26 is the *cumulative frequency* corresponding to 7 marks.

Mark	Frequency	Cumulative frequency
0	0	0
1	1	1
2	2	3
3	2	5
4	3	8
5	5	13
6	7	20
7	6	26
8	4	30
9	3	33
10	2	35

See *data; event; frequency*

cup   A *cup* is a small container for liquids. It is shaped like a bowl and has a small handle. In recipes a *cup* is a measuring unit for liquids:
1 *cup* = 250 ml (millilitres).

See *millilitre*

currency   *Currency* is another term for 'money'. Every country has its own type of *currency*: South Africa has rands (R) and cents (c), Botswana has the pula (P) and thebe (t). Nigeria has the naira (₦) and kobo (k).

See *money*

curve   A *curve* is a line that bends in a continuous way, without angles or straight sections. A line with this property is a *curved* line. A *curved* line always changes direction.
- These are all examples of *curves*:

See *angle; straight line*

curve of constant breadth   A *curve of constant breadth* has the property that when it rolls along a flat surface, the point at the top of the curve is always the same height above the surface.

• A circle is an example of *curve of constant breadth*.

cyclic quadrilateral   When a circle can be drawn through all four corners (vertices) of a quadrilateral, the quadrilateral is called a *cyclic quadrilateral*. The word 'cyclic' means 'like a circle'.

• This is a *cyclic quadrilateral*:

• This is not a *cyclic quadrilateral*:

See *quadrilateral; vertex*

cycloid   A *cycloid* is the curved path of a point on the perimeter (circumference) of a circle as the circle rolls along a straight line.

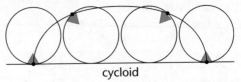

cycloid

See *circle; circumference; perimeter*

cylinder, cylindrical   A *cylinder* is a three-dimensional object. Its top and bottom faces are circles and its cross-sections are all circles of the same radius. A *cylinder* can be solid like a sausage, or hollow like an empty tin can. An object with this shape is described as a *cylindrical* object.

See *circle; cross-section; radius; three-dimensional*

D

daily wage   A *wage* is money that a worker is paid for the work he or she does. A *daily wage* is the wage that the worker gets for one day's work.
- John gets a *daily wage* of R200 for his work at the car park.

See *salary*

data   *Data* are collections of information in number form. These number facts are collected by researchers who want to find out how often something happens, or how many people do different things, or how something changes from year to year. *Data* is a plural noun. The singular form is 'datum', which means 'one number fact'.
- Researchers collected *data* about how people travel to work every morning. They wanted to find out how many people travel alone in their cars, how many people travel by taxi or cycle, and how many people take the bus or the train to work. They will use these *data* to plan better transport systems for the city.

See *statistics*

database   A *database* is a large collection of data (number facts) about a particular subject, which is stored on a computer or in a filing system. The people who own the database can use it to help them organise and plan their work.
- The headmaster of a school keeps a *database* of all the learners' names, home addresses, ages, and the learning areas they study.

See *data; statistics*

date   A *date* is a number that describes a particular day in a particular month and year.
- Everyone looks forward to the *date* when the school holidays start.
- South Africa's first democratic election was held on 27 April 1994. This is a very important *date* in our history.

See *day; month; year*

day   A *day* is the time it takes for the Earth to turn once on its own axis through darkness (night time) and light (daytime). A *day* on Earth is 24 hours long. There are seven *days* in one week. The *days* of the week are: Monday, Tuesday, Wednesday, Thursday, Friday, Saturday and Sunday.

See *hour*

debt   A *debt* is something that you owe to someone else. A *debt* can be money, or it can be something else that you have borrowed and must give back.
- Olivia has many *debts*. She has borrowed money from all her friends to buy things. Now she must pay back the money or her friends will be angry.

decade   A *decade* is a period of ten years. 'Deca–' comes from the Latin word for 'ten'.
- The *decade* from 1990 to 1999 was a very important time in South Africa's history.

decagon A *decagon* is a polygon with ten sides. 'Deca–' comes from the Latin word for 'ten'. When all its sides and angles are equal, it is called a regular decagon.

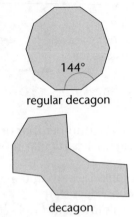

144°

regular decagon

decagon

See *polygon*

decimal, decimal system *Decimal* describes things that are grouped in tens. We use a *decimal system* for counting and calculating with numbers: units, tens, hundreds, thousands, and so on. *Decimals* can be multiples of 10: 10, 100, 1 000, 10 000, ... or divisions of 10: $\frac{1}{10}, \frac{1}{100}, \frac{1}{1\,000}, \frac{1}{10\,000}$, ...

- Our measuring units are based on *decimals*:
  1 centimetre = 10 millimetres
  1 metre = 100 centimetres
  1 kilometre = 1 000 metres

See *decimal fraction; decimal number*

decimal comma The *decimal comma* is the symbol that separates whole numbers from the decimal fractions in a decimal number. In some cases, a decimal point is used instead of a *decimal comma*, for example, bank statements and till slips all have decimal points.

- The *decimal comma* comes between the units and the tenths in these decimal fractions:
  12,3
  1,345
  100,006

See *comma; decimal fraction; decimal number*

decimal fraction A *decimal fraction* is a fraction in which the denominator is a power. In a common fraction you write the numerator and the denominator of the fraction, but in a *decimal fraction* you only write the numerator part of the fraction, with a comma between the whole number and the numerator part of the number.

- The common fraction $\frac{25}{100}$ can be written as the *decimal fraction* 0,25.
- The common fraction $2\frac{3}{10}$ can be written as the *decimal fraction* 2,3.

See *common fraction; decimal number*

decimal notation *Decimal notation* is a way of writing numbers that uses decimal commas to show the fraction part of the number, instead of numerators and denominators.

- To write $673\frac{3}{4}$ in *decimal notation*, first change the fraction $\frac{3}{4}$ into a fraction with a denominator that is a multiple of 10:
  $\frac{3}{4} = \frac{75}{100}$
  Then write the number with a decimal comma before the fraction part:
  $673\frac{3}{4} = 673,75$

See *decimal fraction; decimal number*

decimal number A *decimal number* is a number that is written in base 10 notation. Values to the left of the decimal comma are whole numbers, and each place value represents a power of 10. Values to the right of the decimal comma are fractions, and each place value represents a power of $\frac{1}{10}$.

See *decimal*

decimal places The number of *decimal places* in a decimal number is the number of values to the right of the comma. When you do calculations with decimal numbers, you sometimes round off the answer to one, two or three *decimal places*, using the rules for rounding off numbers.

- The number 4,1247832 has seven *decimal places*.
  If we round off this number to three *decimal places* we get 4,125.

See *decimal comma; decimal number; round off*

decrease To *decrease* means to become less, or to make something smaller.
- During summer in Cape Town, the rain *decreases* – there is less rain than in winter.
- Sipho must *decrease* his expenses. He spends about R5 000 every month but he only earns R4 500.

deduct To *deduct* something means to take it away or subtract it.
- I borrowed R100 from my employer. He will *deduct* R10 from my wages every week until I have paid him back.

See *subtract*

definition A *definition* of something is an accurate description of what it is, and what its properties are.
- The *definition* of a square is a polygon with four sides of equal length and four right angles.

See *properties*

degree *Degrees* are units for measuring the size of angles, or the amount of turn. One complete turn is 360 *degrees* (360°). The symbol for *degrees* is °. The system of 360° for one turn is based on the system that was first developed by the ancient Mesopotamians, who divided a circle into 360 equal parts. (One complete turn makes the shape of a circle.)
- The arrow starts off facing east.
  - If it is turned left to north, it turns 90°.
  - If it continues to west, it turns 180°.
  - If it continues to south, it turns 270°.
  - If it turns right around and ends back at east, it turns 360°.

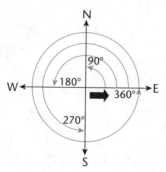

See *angle*

degree of a polynomial The *degree of a polynomial* is the highest power of the variable in the polynomial. Polynomials of degree 2 are called quadratic polynomials, and polynomials of degree 3 are called cubic polynomials.
- The *degree of the polynomial* $2x^6 + 3x^4 - 5x^3 + x + 8$ is 6.

See *polynomial; power of a number; variable*

delete To *delete* something means to remove it or cross it out.
- If you *delete* all the vowels from this sentence, you are left with:
  f y *dlt* ll th vwls frm ths sntnc, y r lft wth.

See *cross out*

demand 1. To *demand* means to ask for something in a very firm way.
2. The *demand* for goods is the want or need that people have for these goods.
- The teacher *demands* to see Salim's homework.
- The *demand* for Christmas trees is very high in December.

denary The *denary* system is the base 10 number system.

See *base; decimal system*

denominator The *denominator* is the number below the dividing line in a fraction. The *denominator* shows how many equal parts the whole has been divided into for the fraction.
- In the fraction $\frac{3}{4}$, 4 is the *denominator*. It shows that the whole has been divided into four equal parts.

See *numerator*

dependent events Two events are *dependent events* when one depends on (is affected by) the other.
- Suppose a bag contains 4 red beads and 6 black beads. A bead is drawn from the bag. This is the first event. Then a second bead is drawn. This is the second event. The chance of the second bead being red depends on the colour of the first bead that was taken from the bag. These two events are *dependent events*.

See *event*

dependent variable   A *dependent variable* is a variable whose value will depend on (be affected by) the value of another variable called the independent variable.
- This graph show how the average female baby's height changes as its age increases. The baby's height is a *dependent variable* – it depends on how old the baby is.

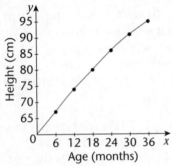

See *independent variable*

deposit   To *deposit* money means to pay it into a bank or building society for safekeeping.
- At the end of every day, the shopkeeper *deposits* her money from sales into her bank account.

See *withdraw*

depreciate   1. To *depreciate* something is to consider it of little value.
2. In mathematical terms, something *depreciates* if its money value decreases over time.

See *appreciate*

depth   *Depth* is a measure of how deep something is. It is the distance below the surface.
- The *depth* of the sea at this point is 60 metres.

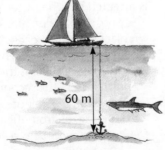

60 m

descend   To *descend* means to go down, or to decrease in value.
- The numbers *descend* from 100 to 90:
  100, 99, 98, 97, 96, 95, 94, 93, 92, 91, 90

See *ascend*

descending order   To arrange numbers in *descending order* means to arrange them from the biggest number to the smallest number.
- If we arrange 39, 83, 102, 27, 44 in *descending order* we get:
  102, 83, 44, 39, 27

See *ascending order*

describe   To *describe* something means to say what it is, what its properties are and what it does, using words or pictures.
- You can *describe* a circle using words or a diagram with labels:

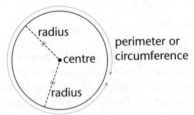

A circle is a round two-dimensional shape in which all the points on the perimeter are the same distance from the centre.

See *properties*

description   A *description* is a statement that tells you what a particular object is, what its properties are and what it does.
- This is a *description* of an ostrich:
  'An ostrich is a bird. It has long legs, a very long neck and a tiny head. Its wings are big but it cannot fly. It lays enormous eggs. One ostrich egg is about the same size as 24 hen's eggs. An ostrich can run very fast. It can kill an animal or person with its strong kick.'

determine To *determine* something means to find out the exact information or the exact answer. It can also mean to make a decision about something.

diagonal A *diagonal* is a straight line that goes from any corner (vertex) of a shape to any other corner of the shape (except a corner right next to it). Polygons and polyhedra can have *diagonals*.
- This rectangle has 2 *diagonals*:

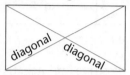

See *polygon; polyhedron*

diagram A *diagram* is an accurate drawing that shows the parts of a shape or an object.
- This is a *diagram* of a triangle:

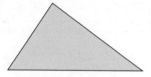

diameter A *diameter* of a circle is a straight line through the centre of the circle that joins two points on the circumference. The *diameter* is equal to twice the length of the radius. Each *diameter* is a line of symmetry that divides the circle into two semi-circles.

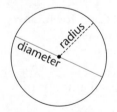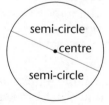

See *circle; circumference; line of symmetry; radius*

difference The *difference* between two numbers is the size of the gap between them. We find the *difference* by subtracting the smaller number from the bigger number.

- Find the *difference* between 18 and 24: 24 − 18 = 6. Therefore the *difference* between 18 and 24 is 6.
- Find the *difference* between −7 and −15: −7 − (−15) = −7 + 15 = 8. Therefore the *difference* between −7 and −15 is 8.

See *subtraction*

differentiate To *differentiate* between two things is to show the ways in which they are different from each other.
- To *differentiate* between positive and negative integers, we write negative integers with a minus sign and positive integers with an addition sign:
  negative integers: −1; −35; −0,5
  positive integers: +1; +35; +0,5

See *integer*

digit A *digit* is one of the ten number symbols that we use to write all the numbers in our number system: 0, 1, 2, 3, 4, 5, 6, 7, 8, 9
- A three-*digit* number is any number that has three *digits*:
  478, 201, 333 are all three-*digit* numbers.

See *number*

digit sum A *digit sum* is the sum of the digits that form a number.
- The *digit sum* of the number 4 523 is 4 + 5 + 2 + 3 = 14.
- The *digit sum* of the number 101 is 1 + 0 + 1 = 2.

digital clock A *digital clock* tells the time by showing only the numbers for the hours and minutes (and sometimes also seconds). The numbers change every minute (or second) to show the exact time that it is now. A *digital clock* does not have a face and moving hands, like an analogue clock.

See *analogue clock*

digital time *Digital time* is the time that a digital clock shows. Depending on how the clock is set, it could be either 12-hour or 24-hour notation. See the table on page 155 of this dictionary.

See *digital clock*

dimension 1. A *dimension* is a measurement that tells you about the size of a shape or object. Length, breadth and height are all *dimensions* of a shape.
2. The *dimension* of a space is the number of coordinates needed to describe the position of a point (P) in the space. A line is one-dimensional, a plane is two-dimensional and the space we live in is three-dimensional.

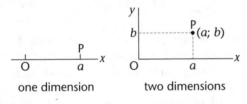

one dimension   two dimensions

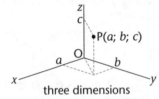

three dimensions

See *coordinates; three-dimensional; two-dimensional*

direct proportion If two quantities are in *direct proportion* to each other, that means that as the one quantity increases or decreases, the other quantity increases or decreases in a similar way.

- Your body mass is in *direct proportion* to the amount of food you eat. The more food you eat, the more body mass you will develop.

- The number of legs on the ladybirds is *directly proportional* to the number of ladybirds:
  1 ladybird has 6 legs.
  2 ladybirds have 12 legs.
  5 ladybirds have 30 legs.

Number of ladybirds	Number of legs
	6
	12
	30

See *indirect proportion*

directed number Positive and negative numbers are called *directed numbers*. When they are represented on a number line, the negative numbers increase to the left from 0, and the positive numbers increase to the right from 0. These directions are important properties of the numbers.

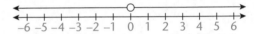

See *number line*

direction A *direction* is a position to which you are going, or from which you are moving away. *Directions* are often described using the compass points north, south, east and west.

- If you travel in the *direction* south-west from Johannesburg, you will eventually get to Cape Town.
- The summer wind in Cape Town blows from the *direction* south-east.

See *compass*

discount A *discount* is an amount of money that is taken off the price of an item in a shop, to give the customer a cheaper price.

discrete variable   A *discrete variable* is a variable that can take only whole-number values.

- The variable 'number of children in the family' can take only whole-number values such as 1, 2, 3, and so on. There cannot be a fraction of a child, or a negative-integer child.

See *continuous variable; variable; whole number*

discuss   To *discuss* a question or problem means to talk about it with other people, to explain and compare your thoughts, and to analyse everyone's suggestions to see which ideas are useful in answering the question or solving the problem.

disjoint sets   Two or more sets are *disjoint sets* if they have no elements in common.

- A is the set of even numbers from 2 to 10:
  A = {2, 4, 6, 8, 10}
  B is the set of odd numbers from 1 to 9:
  B = {1, 3, 5, 7, 9}
  A and B are *disjoint sets* because they have no common elements.

See *element of a set*

displacement   *Displacement* means movement of an object in a particular direction. An object is displaced if it is moved from one position to another.

- The speeding truck knocked over the wheelie bin. This caused *displacement* of the bin, which is now in a different position.

disprove   To *disprove* something means to show that it is not true.

- People used to believe that the Sun moves around Earth, until the astronomer Galileo *disproved* this belief. He proved that Earth moves around the Sun.

distance   The *distance* between two points or positions is a measure of how far apart they are. We measure *distance* in length units like centimetres, metres and kilometres.

- The *distance* between Durban and Johannesburg by road is 811 kilometres. The *distance* by air is less than this because the plane does not have to follow all the curves of a road.

distribute equally   To *distribute equally* means to divide something into equal portions (pieces) and give each person the same amount of the thing.

- When you bake muffins, you must *distribute* the muffin mixture *equally* among all the muffin pans.

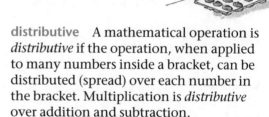

distributive   A mathematical operation is *distributive* if the operation, when applied to many numbers inside a bracket, can be distributed (spread) over each number in the bracket. Multiplication is *distributive* over addition and subtraction.

- $6 \times (7 + 3 + 4) = (6 \times 7) + (6 \times 3) + (6 \times 4) = 42 + 18 + 24 = 84$
- $6 \times (20 - 5 - 7) = (6 \times 20) - (6 \times 5) - (6 \times 7) = 120 - 30 - 42 = 48$

diverge   A sequence of numbers *diverges* if it increases at regular intervals.

- The sequence 1, 2, 4, 8, 16, 32, … *diverges*. Each term in the sequence is double the term before it.
- The sequence $\frac{1}{2}, \frac{3}{4}, \frac{7}{8}, \frac{15}{16}, \frac{31}{32},$ … does not *diverge*.

See *converge; sequence*

divide, division   To *divide* something means to break it up into parts. When you *divide* one number into another number, you are finding out how many times the first number fits into the second number. This is called *division*.

- *Divide* 12 by 4:
  $12 \div 4 = 3$
  This means that 4 'fits into' 12 three times.

dividend In a division calculation, the number that is being divided into equal parts is called the *dividend*.

• In the division calculation 12 ÷ 4, 12 is the *dividend*.

See *divide; divisor*

divisible A natural number is divisible by another natural number if it can be divided by that number without remainders. So 12 is *divisible* by 3 because 12 = 3 × 4. 10 is not *divisible* by 3.

divisibility rules *Divisibility rules* are quick ways to check whether one number can be divided by another number without leaving any remainder.

• Some *divisibility rules* are:
  ‣ Any whole number ending in 0 or 5 is divisible by 5.
  ‣ Any even whole number is divisible by 2.
  ‣ Any whole number whose digit sum is divisible by 3 or 9 is itself divisible by 3 or 9.

See *divide*

divisor In a division calculation, the number that is divided into another number is called the *divisor*.

• In the division calculation 12 ÷ 4, 4 is the *divisor*.

See *divide; dividend*

dodecagon A *dodecagon* is a polygon with 12 sides. 'Dodeca–' means '12'.

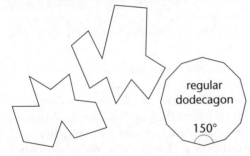

regular dodecagon

150°

See *polygon*

dodecahedron A *dodecahedron* is a polyhedron with 12 faces. Each face is a regular pentagon.

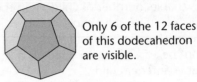

Only 6 of the 12 faces of this dodecahedron are visible.

See *dodecagon; polyhedron*

domain The *domain* of a function is the set of elements (possible *x*-values) on which the function operates.

• The function $f(x) = x^2 - 3$ operates on the set of elements {−3, −2, −1, 0, 1, 2, 3}.

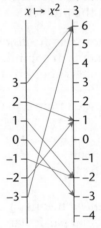

$x \mapsto x^2 - 3$

{−3, −2, −1, 0, 1, 2, 3} is the *domain* of the function.

See *function*

dot A *dot* is a small round mark on the page that represents a point in space. A point has no length, breadth or height – we cannot show this on the page so we use the smallest possible pen or pencil mark to represent the point.

• Can you see this *dot*?   •

See *point*

dotted line A *dotted line* is a line made up of dots. It can be used to show the position that a line or edge can have, when the line or edge is not yet in that position.

- The *dotted lines* on the card show where you need to fold the card to make a box.

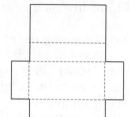

dotty rectangles   *Dotty rectangles* are dots arranged in patterns of rectangular shapes.

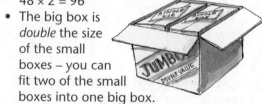

See *rectangle*

double   To *double* something means to multiply it by two. A shape is *double* the size of another shape if it is twice as big as the first shape.
- If you *double* 48 you get 96:
  48 × 2 = 96
- The big box is *double* the size of the small boxes – you can fit two of the small boxes into one big box.

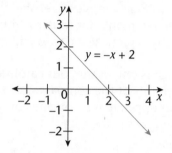

down, downwards   To move *down* or *downwards* means to move to a lower position than you were in before.
- The girl climbs *down* the tree.
- If you look at the graph from left to right you can see that it is sloping *downwards*.

$$y = -x + 2$$

dozen   A *dozen* is a group of 12 things.
- Nthabiseng bought a *dozen* hot cross buns for Easter Sunday.

See *baker's dozen*

duodecimal numbers   Numbers in base 12 are called *duodecimal numbers*. They are expressed using groupings of units, twelves, (twelve)^2, (twelve)^3, etc.

See *base*

duration   The *duration* of something is the length of time that it lasts.
- The *duration* of the school term is 10 weeks.
- The *duration* of a soccer match is 90 minutes.

E

earn To *earn* money means to get money in exchange for work that you do.

- Lebo works in a music store. She *earns* R3 500 per month for working from 9 a.m. to 5 p.m., Monday to Friday.

east *East* is one of the four cardinal (main) points of the compass. It is the direction opposite west on the compass.

- The sun rises in the *east*.

See *compass*

edge The *edge* of a shape is where two faces of the shape meet (touch each other). An *edge* can be straight or curved. Different shapes have different numbers of *edges*.

- A cube has 12 *edges*.

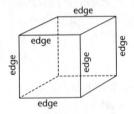

- A triangular prism has 9 *edges*.

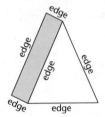

See *face*

eighth One *eighth* is one part of a whole that has been divided into eight equal parts called *eighths*. The number symbol for this fraction is $\frac{1}{8}$.

$\frac{1}{8}$	$\frac{1}{8}$	$\frac{1}{8}$	$\frac{1}{8}$
$\frac{1}{8}$	$\frac{1}{8}$	$\frac{1}{8}$	$\frac{1}{8}$

See *fraction*

element of a set The individual members of a set are called the *elements of a set*. The symbol ∈ means 'is an element of'.

- If the set A = {days of the week}, then the *elements* of A are Monday, Tuesday, Wednesday, Thursday, Friday, Saturday, Sunday. There are seven elements in this set. We can write the statement 'Wednesday is an *element of the set* A' in the form 'Wednesday ∈ A'.
- If the set B = {even numbers between 1 and 21} then the *elements of set* B are 2, 4, 6, 8, 10, 12, 14, 16, 18, 20. There are ten elements in this set. We can write the statement '6 is an *element of the set* B' in the form '6 ∈ B'.

See *set*

elevation of a building An *elevation of a building* is a view of the building as seen from the front or the side.

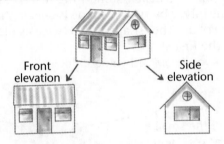

Front elevation   Side elevation

ellipse An *ellipse* is a two-dimensional shape. It is the shape that you get if you cut a cross-section of a cylinder at an angle. You also get an *ellipse* if you stretch a circle in opposite directions.

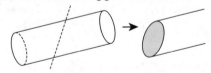

- The shape of the Earth's orbit around the Sun is an *ellipse*.

See *circle; cross-section; cylinder; two-dimensional*

empty set   An *empty set* (also called a *null set*) is a set that has no elements in it. The symbol for an *empty set* is { } or ∅.
- The set F = {days of the week that contain the letter Z} has no elements in it. It is an *empty set*.

See *element of a set*

enlargement   An *enlargement* is a transformation that changes the size of an object without changing its shape.
- The film projector makes an *enlargement* of the picture so that it looks much bigger on the screen.

See *transformation*

equal   Two things are *equal* if they have exactly the same value. The symbol for 'is equal to' is =. This is called the equal sign.
- 3 + 5 = 8 and 2 + 1 + 1 + 4 = 8. Therefore 3 + 5 is *equal* to 2 + 1 + 1 + 4, because they are both *equal* to 8.
- There are *equal* distances between the farms Tweespruit and Winterhoek, and the farms Winterhoek and Kleinrivier.

equally likely   Two things are *equally likely* if the chances of them happening are the same.
- When you toss a coin, it is *equally likely* that it will land heads up or tails up.

equation   An *equation* is a mathematical statement that uses an equal sign (=) to state that one expression is equal to another expression. Any value of the variable in the expression that makes the statement true, is called a solution of the *equation*.
- In the *equation* $3x - 2 = 4$, the value $x = 2$ makes the *equation* true.

equation of a line   Every straight line can be described by an *equation of the line* with variables x and y. When pairs of coordinates $(x; y)$ that are solutions of the equation are plotted as points on the graph, they can be joined to form the straight line.

- $y = x - 4$ is the *equation of a line*. The coordinate pairs (0; –4), (4; 0), (5; 1) and (6; 2) are all solutions of this equation. If these coordinates are plotted on a Cartesian plane, they can be joined to form a straight line.

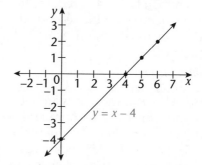

See *Cartesian plane; coordinates*

equilateral, equilateral triangle   An *equilateral* shape is a shape with sides of equal length. An *equilateral triangle* is a triangle with all three sides the same length.

See *triangle*

equilibrium   *Equilibrium* is a state of being in balance. A balance scale is *in equilibrium* if the items on each of its pans are equal in mass.

equivalent   Two or more number values are *equivalent* if they can be rewritten in a form that shows that they have the same value.
- 10^2 is *equivalent* to 25 × 4 because $10^2 = 100$ and 25 × 4 = 100.

equivalent fractions   *Equivalent fractions* are fractions that can all be cancelled to the same simplest form.
- $\frac{2}{3}, \frac{4}{6}, \frac{6}{9}, \frac{10}{15}$ and $\frac{14}{21}$ are all *equivalent fractions*. They can all be written in the same simplest form: $\frac{2}{3}$.

See *cancel; fraction*

equivalent ratios   Two ratios are *equivalent ratios* when they can be reduced to the same numbers by division or multiplication of a common factor.
- 8 : 20 and 6 : 15 are *equivalent ratios*. If the numbers in the first ratio are divided by the common factor 4, it reduces to 2 : 5. If the numbers in the second ratio are divided by the common factor 3, it also reduces to 2 : 5.

See *common factor*

equivalent sets   *Equivalent sets* are sets that have the same cardinal number – that is, the same number of elements.
- The set S = {3, 6, 9, 12, 15} and the set T = {apple, banana, orange, plum, cherry} are *equivalent sets* because they both have five elements – that is, they both have the cardinal number 5.

See *cardinal number; element of a set*

error   An *error* is a mistake, or an inaccurate calculation.
- Can you spot the *error* in this addition calculation?
  33 + 44 + 111 = 88

See *mistake*

establish   To *establish* something means to prove that it is true.
- Scientists have *established* that there is no oxygen on the moon. Therefore anyone who walks on the moon must use oxygen tanks to breathe.

estimate   To *estimate* the answer to a problem, you judge what the answer will be without doing any measurement or calculation. You use your knowledge of the situation to help you judge – estimating is not the same as guessing.
- Mr Damon is a very experienced tailor. He can *estimate* how much cloth he will need to make a suit for you, even before he measures the exact length of your arms and legs.

evaluate   To *evaluate* means to find the value of something.
- *Evaluate* $32xy^2$ when $x = 5$ and $y = 4$:
  $$32xy^2 = 32 \times 5 \times 4^2$$
  $$= 32 \times 5 \times 16$$
  $$= 2\,560$$

even numbers   *Even numbers* are numbers that are multiples of 2. Any number that has 2 as a factor is even. Every number that ends in 0, 2, 4, 6, or 8 is even.
- 2, 4, 6, 8, 10, 12, … are *even numbers*.
- 3 954 is even, but 24 683 is odd.

See *odd numbers*

evens   *Evens* is the name given to the probability of any event that has a 50% chance of happening.
- When a coin is tossed, there is an equal chance (a 50% chance) of it landing with heads or tails showing. So the probability of getting heads or tails for each coin toss is *evens*.

See *probability*

event   An *event* is the term used in statistics to describe something whose probability you are looking for.
- There are five names in a hat and you are drawing one particular name from the hat. This is called an *event*. The probability of drawing one particular name from the hat is 1 in 5 or $\frac{1}{5}$.

See *probability*

examine   To *examine* something means to study it in detail, investigate its properties or find out how it works. Examination can be done by asking questions, by testing how the object works, or by taking it apart to study the pieces.
- In the science classroom, learners often *examine* insects.

example   An *example* is a model or
sample of something that shows how
it looks or how it works.
- This is an *example* of an arithmetic
  calculation with multiplication and
  subtraction. When you have studied it,
  make up three calculations of your own
  with these operations and find their
  solutions.
  Example:
  $$31 \times 56 - 7 \times 11 - 9 \times 66$$
  $$= 1\ 736 - 77 - 594 \text{ (first multiply, then}$$
  $$\text{subtract)}$$
  $$= 1\ 065$$

exchange   To *exchange* something
means to give it to someone and get
something back in return. We usually
exchange money for goods in a shop.
- This skirt doesn't fit me. I want to
  exchange it for a smaller size.
- Nina painted her friend Pumezo's fence,
  and in *exchange* Pumezo fixed Nina's
  broken shed.

exchange rate   Every country has its
own type of money, called currency.
When you travel from one country to
another you need to exchange your
own currency for the currency of that
country. The rate at which you can buy
that currency (how much it costs in your
own currency) is called the *exchange rate*.
The *exchange rate* between two currencies
changes all the time.
- If the *exchange rate* for US dollars in
  South Africa is $1 = R6,40 this means
  that every dollar you buy will cost you
  R6,40. If you have R10 000 to exchange,
  this will buy you $\frac{10\ 000}{6,40}$ = $1 562,50.

See *currency*

exercise   An *exercise* is a task that you do
to practise a method or skill that you
have learnt.
- Yesterday the class learned how to draw
  straight-line graphs. Today they are
  doing *exercises* to practise drawing
  graphs.

expand   To *expand* an algebraic
expression means to multiply out the
brackets in the expression. The
distributive law is used to *expand*
expressions with brackets.
- *Expand $a(b + c)$*.
  $$a(b + c) = ab + ac$$
- *Expand $(2x + 3)(x - 1)$*.
  $$(2x + 3)(x - 1) = 2x(x - 1) + 3(x - 1)$$
  $$= 2x^2 - 2x + 3x - 3$$
  $$= 2x^2 + x - 3$$

See *algebra; distributive; expression*

expanded notation   *Expanded notation* is
a way of writing a number so that the
value of each digit in the number is
shown separately.
- If we write the number 24 689 in
  expanded notation we get:
  20 000 + 4 000 + 600 + 80 + 9.

expansion   *Expansion* is the act of
getting bigger. It can also mean the
expression that you get when you
expand an algebraic expression.
- The *expansion* of $a(b + c)$
  is $ab + ac$.
- The *expansion* of the city happens when
  more and more people come to live
  there.

See *expand*

explain   To *explain* something means to
give reasons why it happens.
- The farmers *explain* the bad harvest by
  saying that there was not enough rain
  this year to keep the young plants alive.

explanation   An *explanation* is a set of
reasons why something happens.
- The *explanation* for the cholera problem
  in this settlement is that people have no
  access to clean water in their houses.
  They must use the river water to cook
  and wash with, even though it is full of
  dirt and germs.

See *explain*

explore   To *explore* something means to study it or investigate it without knowing what you could find there, or what you might have to do.

• The children decided to *explore* the cave, even though they did not know if there was a wild animal living inside it.

exponent   An *exponent* is another word for the power of a number. If a number is raised to a certain power, this power is called the *exponent* of the number.

• If 3 is raised to the power 2, then the *exponent* of 3 is 2 (3^2). 3 is called the base. $3^2 = 3 \times 3 = 9$.

See *base; power of a number*

exponential, exponential function
A quantity changes (increases or decreases) in an *exponential* way if it is raised by a certain exponent. A *function* is *exponential* if it can be written as an expression that includes an exponent.

• Suppose a population of bacteria doubles in size every hour. If its population was 100 when it was first seen, then the population P after t hours is given by the *exponential function* $P = 100 \times 2^t$.

See *exponent; function*

expression   An *expression* is a set of connected mathematical symbols.

• These are all examples of *expressions*:
  ‣ $5xy^2$
  ‣ $3x + 4x^4 - xyz$
  ‣ $\left(\frac{1}{2}b\right)^3$
  ‣ $\sqrt{a^2 + b^2}$

extend   To *extend* something means to make it longer.

• To draw the altitude from the vertex A of this triangle, you need to *extend* the line BC opposite vertex A.

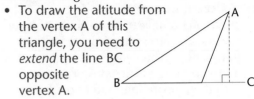

See *altitude of a triangle*

exterior angle   An *exterior angle* is the angle that you get when you extend a side of a polygon beyond the vertex. It is the angle outside the polygon between this extended side and another side of the polygon. 'Exterior' means 'outside'.

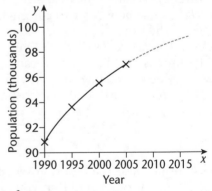

See *polygon; vertex*

extrapolate   To *extrapolate* means to use information (data) that you already know, to predict the values of data outside the range of what you know.

• Town planners use the population numbers up to the present that they have collected, to predict what the population is likely to be in the future. They are *extrapolating* from known population data to help them plan for the future needs of the population.

See *data*

extremes   See *outlier*

F

face A *face* is the flat side of a polygon. The *faces* meet at edges.
• This triangular prism has five *faces*. Three of the *faces* are rectangular and two *faces* are triangular.

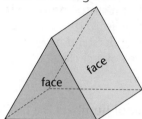

See *edge; polygon; triangular prism*

face of a clock See *clock face*

fact A *fact* is a piece of information that we know is true.
• It is a *fact* that the Sun rises in the east and sets in the west.

factor A *factor* of a number is another number that divides into the first number exactly (without any remainder).
• The *factors* of 6 are 1, 2, 3 and 6.
  1 divides into 6 six times: $6 \div 1 = 6$
  2 divides into 6 three times: $6 \div 2 = 3$
  3 divides into 6 two times: $6 \div 3 = 2$
  6 divides into 6 once: $6 \div 6 = 1$

See *common factor; divide*

factorise To *factorise* a number or an algebraic expression means to write it as a product of its factors.
• We can *factorise* 10 as 2×5 or 10×1.
• The algebraic expression $pq + ps$ can be *factorised* as $p(q + s)$.

See *algebraic expression; product*

Fahrenheit Degrees *Fahrenheit* are units that can be used to measure the temperature of something (how hot or cold it is). The measuring unit is written as °F.

In South Africa we use degrees Celsius (°C) as measuring units for temperature.
• 0 °C (freezing point) is the same as 32 °F. 100 °C (boiling point for water) is the same as 212 °F.

See *Celsius; thermometer*

false A statement is *false* if it is wrong or untrue.
• It is *false* to say that only tall people are good at sport. Some of the best athletes in the world are short people.

See *true*

far Two places or objects are *far* from each other if the distance or length between them is big.
• The planet Jupiter is very *far* away from the Sun – nearly 780 million kilometres.

See *near*

few *Few* means a small quantity of something, not many things.
• There are lots of apples in the bowl but only a *few* bananas.

Fibonacci sequence The *Fibonacci sequence* is the set of numbers 0, 1, 1, 2, 3, 5, 8, 13, 21, … in which each number from the third number onwards is the sum of the previous two numbers. The sequence is named after the Italian mathematician Leonardo Fibonacci who discovered the sequence.
• The fourth number in the sequence is 3, which is equal to the sum of the previous two numbers, $1 + 2$.
• The seventh number in the sequence is 13, which is the sum of the previous two numbers, $5 + 8$.

See *sequence*

fifth   1. A *fifth* is one of five equal parts of a whole.
2. The *fifth* item in a list is the item that comes after the first four items.
- The circle is divided into five equal parts. One fifth $\left(\frac{1}{5}\right)$ is shaded.

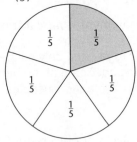

figure   1. A *figure* is another word for the symbol that is used to write a number.
2. A *figure* is a diagram or sketch of an object or shape.
- Seventy-two written in *figures* is 72.
- In the *figure* below, find the value of *x*.

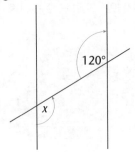

fill in   To *fill in* a word or number means to write in the missing word or number in a sentence or calculation.
- *Fill in* the missing values in these addition calculations:

  3 + ___ = 21

  34 + 102 = ___

final   The *final* item in a group is the item at the end of the group. The *final* number in a series is the number at the end of the series.
- The *final* game of the World Cup soccer tournament will decide which team is the best in the world.

financial   *Financial* information is information about money and business matters.
- The *financial* pages of the newspaper are full of information about what is happening in the business world.

finish   To *finish* something means to come to the end of it or to complete it.
- When you have *finished* the activity on circles, you will understand how to calculate the area of a circle.

See *complete (verb)*

finite   A *finite* set of numbers is a limited set.
- The set of odd numbers between 0 and 12 is a *finite* set. It has six elements: {1, 3, 5, 7, 9, 11}.
  The set of all odd numbers is not finite because it is unlimited.

See *infinite set*

first   The *first* item in a group is the item at the beginning of the group.
- The *first* letter in the alphabet is A.

See *final; last*

fixed deposit   A *fixed deposit* is an amount of money (a deposit) that you leave in a bank account for a fixed (unchanging) time period. This is a type of savings account.
- Tshepo put his money in a *fixed deposit* account for six months. He will earn 7% interest on this money. He cannot get the money out of the account until the six months are over.

See *bank account*

flat   A *flat* shape is a shape that has length and breadth, but no height.
- Squares, triangles and circles are examples of *flat* shapes. All polygons are *flat* shapes.

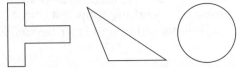

See *polygon*

flow diagram, flow chart   A *flow diagram* or *flow chart* is a diagram that shows how different actions follow one after the other. It can be used to give a set of step-by-step instructions to solve a problem, or to show how the different parts of an activity are organised.

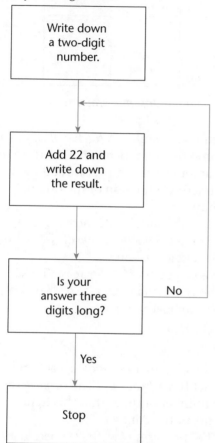

foot   A *foot* is a unit of measurement of length. It is part of the imperial system of measuring units. 1 *foot* is equal to approximately 30 centimetres.

foot of the perpendicular   The *foot of the perpendicular* is the point where the perpendicular line forms a right angle with another line.

• In the diagram, D is the *foot of the perpendicular* from A to BC.

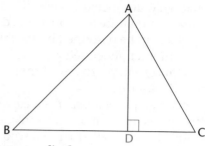

See *perpendicular*

foreign exchange   *Foreign exchange* is another way of referring to foreign currency – the types of money that are used in other countries.
• There are laws that limit how much *foreign exchange* you are allowed to buy with South African money.

See *currency; exchange rate*

formula   A *formula* is a general mathematical rule that is expressed using algebraic symbols.
• The *formula* for calculating the area of a triangle A is $A = \frac{1}{2}bh$.
  This is an algebraic way of stating the rule: 'The area of a triangle is equal to half the product of the base and the height of the triangle.'

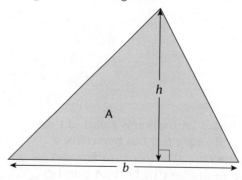

See *algebra*

fractal A *fractal* is a type of curve that has the same degree of regularity, no matter at what distance it is viewed. Many shapes in nature are constructed in ways that can be described by *fractal* curves. Computer-generated graphics often use *fractal* curves to create their shapes and patterns.

- A simple example of a *fractal* is a curve called the Koch snowflake curve (named after the Swedish mathematician who first described it, Helge von Koch). To see how it is constructed, do the following:
  1. Draw an equilateral triangle.
  2. Construct equilateral triangles on the middle third of each side of this triangle, to form a six-pointed star.
  3. Now construct equilateral triangles on each side of the star.
  4. This process can be continued indefinitely.

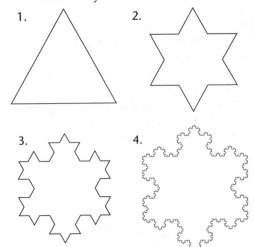

fraction A *fraction* is a part of the whole. A *fraction* has two parts, a numerator (the top number) and a denominator (the bottom number): $\frac{numerator}{denominator}$. The denominator shows into how many equal parts the whole is divided. The numerator shows how many of these parts are in the *fraction*.

- If you divide a square into four equal parts, each part is one fourth or quarter $\left(\frac{1}{4}\right)$ of the whole square. In the diagram below, three parts of the square are shaded – this is the *fraction* $\frac{3}{4}$ of the whole square.

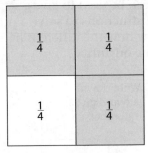

See *denominator; numerator*

fractional change A *fractional change* in an amount is an increase or decrease in the amount that you get by adding or subtracting a fraction of the original amount.

- If an amount of R100 increases by R20, this is a *fractional change* of $\frac{20}{100}$ or $\frac{1}{5}$ of the original amount.
- If an amount of R40 increases by R20, this is a *fractional change* of $\frac{20}{40}$ or $\frac{1}{2}$ of the original amount.

See *fraction*

frequency In a set of data, each item in the set has a *frequency*. The *frequency* is the number of times that this item occurs in the data set.

- The shoe sizes of all the learners in a class are collected. In this set of data, the shoe size 8 occurs 12 times (because 12 learners wear size 8 shoes). The *frequency* of the shoe size 8 is therefore 12.

Shoe size	Tally	Frequency
5	||	2
6	Ⅲ⅂	5
7	ⅢⅢ ||	7
8	ⅢⅢ ⅢⅢ ||	(12)
9	ⅢⅢ |||	8
10	||	2
		36

See *data*

front   1. The *front* of an object is the part that faces forwards.
2. To stand at the *front* of the queue means to stand before (ahead of) the other people in the queue.
3. To stand in *front* of the class means to stand facing everyone in the class.

- Lulu is standing at the *front* of the queue.
- You do your oral in *front* of the class.

See *behind*

full   A container is *full* if there is no more space in it for anything to be added.

- 'You cannot pour more water into that bottle – it is already *full*.'

function   A *function* is a mathematical rule connecting two sets in such a way that for each item (value) in the first set, there is only one item (value) in the second set that is related to it. The first set of a *function* is called the domain, and the second set is called the range.
A *function* is often given a letter name, such as f or g.

- The *function* 'x is multiplied by 3 to give $3x$' can be written in the form:
  $f(x) = 3x$.
  This means that for any value of x in the domain set, there will be one value in the range set that is equal to $3x$.

G

gallon A *gallon* is a measuring unit of capacity (volume) in the imperial system of measurement. 1 *gallon* ≈ 4,55 litres.

See *capacity; imperial units; litre*

generalise To *generalise* means to make a statement about a certain mathematical property that is true for all numbers or situations, not just for a particular number or situation.

• If we multiply 3 × 2 we get an even number, 6.
  If we multiply 217 × 2 we get an even number, 434.
  We can *generalise* this property of numbers by saying that, for any whole number *n*, 2*n* will be an even number.

See *even numbers*

geometric sequence (geometric progression) A *geometric sequence* is a sequence in which a constant ratio exists between consecutive terms.

• The sequence 1, 2, 4, 8, 16, ... is a *geometric sequence* because the difference between any two consecutive terms can be expressed by the ratio 1 : 2.

See *sequence*

geometry *Geometry* is the study of the properties of shapes and space. The word *geometry* comes from the Greek words 'geo', which means 'earth', and 'metry', which means 'measurement'.

• The study of properties of circles, polygons and polyhedra is all part of *geometry*.

See *polygon; polyhedron*

glide reflection A *glide reflection* is a transformation of a shape in which the shape is translated and reflected in a line parallel to the translation.

• Some strip patterns on belts, wallpaper, or pottery use *glide reflection*.

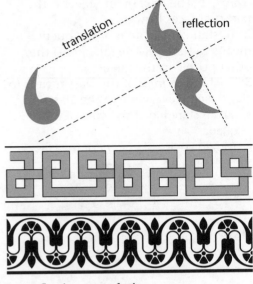

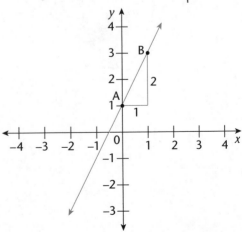

See *reflection; translation*

gradient A *gradient* is the measure of a grade or slope. It can be obtained by taking any two points on the slope, A and B, and dividing the distance up A to B by the distance across A to B:

$$gradient = \frac{\text{distance up}}{\text{distance across}}$$

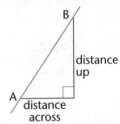

• The *gradient* of the line AB is $\frac{2}{1} = 2$.

gram   A *gram* is a unit for measuring mass. It is approximately the mass of one cubic centimetre of water at 4 °C. The abbreviation for *grams* is 'g'. There are 1 000 *grams* in 1 kilogram.

- A packet of crisps has a mass of 25 *grams*, or 25 g.

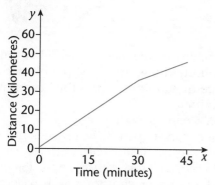

See *metric system*

graph   A *graph* is a way of showing the relationship between two (or more) sets of number values in the form of a picture. A *graph* is usually drawn on a Cartesian plane, with a horizontal axis and a vertical axis.

- This *graph* shows how the distance a car travels changes when it goes at 70 km/h for 30 minutes, and then at 40 km/h for 15 minutes.

See *axis; Cartesian plane*

graphical representation   A *graphical representation* of the solution (answer) to a problem is a way of showing the solution using a graph. The graph shows the relationship between the number values in the problem in such a way that you can find the solution on the graph.

- Find the solution to the equation:
  $x^2 - 4x - 5 = 0$.
  The solution will be the values of x that make the equation true.

A *graphical representation* of the equation is the parabola graph of the equation:

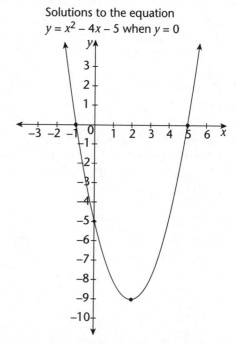

Solutions to the equation
$y = x^2 - 4x - 5$ when $y = 0$

- The solution will be the values of x that make the equation $= 0$ – that is, the values of x where $y = 0$. These values are −1; 0 and 0; 5.

See *parabola*

great circle   A plane that passes through the centre of a sphere intersects the sphere in the shape of a *great circle*.

- Circles of longitude on a globe are *great circles*. The Equator is a circle of latitude that is a *great circle*.

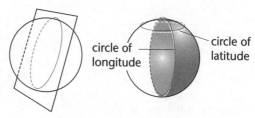

circle of longitude

circle of latitude

See *intersect; plane; sphere*

greater than　A number is *greater than* another number if it has a higher value. The mathematical symbol for *greater than* is >.

- 3 is *greater than* 2.
  1 000 000 is *greater than* 999 999.
  $\frac{1}{2}$ is *greater than* $\frac{15}{75}$.
- 3 > 2.
  1 000 000 > 999 999.
  $\frac{1}{2} > \frac{15}{75}$.

grid paper　*Grid paper* is paper that is printed with vertical and horizontal lines that form squares of equal size. The squares form a grid.

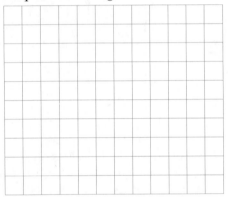

grouped data　When data are collected the numbers in the data are sometimes recorded in groups, also called class intervals. These are *grouped data*.

- When ages of all the learners in a school are recorded, these data can be organised in groups such as:
  7–9 years old
  10–12 years old
  13–15 years old.

Age group	7–9 yrs	10–12 yrs	13–15 yrs
No. of learners	87	69	124

See *class intervals; data*

grouped numbers　*Grouped numbers* are numbers that can be grouped together because they share certain properties.

- Odd numbers form a group; even numbers form a group.

See *even numbers; odd numbers*

H

half　If any number, shape or any object is divided into two equal parts, each part is called a *half* of the whole.

- *Half* of 24 is 12.
- Jeremy and Mpho share the cheese sandwich equally. They each eat *half* the sandwich.

See *fraction*

half full　A container is *half full* if it contains enough liquid or solids to fill half its space.

- This 1-litre jug is only *half full*: it contains 500 ml of milk.

half hour　A *half hour* is a period of time 30 minutes long. 'Half past the hour' is the point 30 minutes after the beginning of an hour.

- On Mondays to Thursdays the supermarket opens at half past eight (08:30) and closes at half past five (17:30). On Fridays it stays open for an extra *half hour*, and closes at six o'clock in the evening (18:00).

See *hour*

half line　A line extends indefinitely in two directions – that is, it goes on forever to the left and to the right. This is sometimes shown by dashes at each end of the line, or by arrowheads at each end. A *half line* has one end point and extends forever in one direction. This is shown by an arrowhead or dashes at one end, and a point (dot) at the other end.

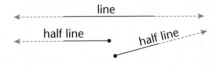

half turn   A *half turn* is a rotation (turn) through 180° – that is, half a circle (which is a 360° turn).

- The angle of a straight line is a *half turn*, that is 180°.

180°
----------------------•----------------------
↘centre of rotation

- If you make a *half turn* you will be facing in the opposite direction to where you were facing before.

See *rotation*

halve   To *halve* something means to divide it into two equal parts. To *halve* a number means to find the value of half the number.

- If Lindiwe and Dumisa both clean the windows, this will *halve* the amount of work that they must each do.
- If you *halve* 350 you get $\frac{350}{2} = 175$.

hand (of a clock)   The *hands* of a clock are the pointers on the face of an analogue clock. The short *hand* shows the hour and the long *hand* shows the minutes.

- The *hands* of the clock show that it is about seven minutes past ten.

See *analogue clock*

heavy   A *heavy* object is an object that is hard to lift or to carry, because of its great mass.

- This piano is really *heavy*! It will take at least four people to lift it.

See *light; mass*

hectare   A *hectare* is a metric measuring unit of area. One *hectare* is equal to 10 000 square metres – that is, a square with length 100 metres and breadth 100 metres. The abbreviation for *hectares* is ha.

- This piece of land is 1 *hectare* (1 ha). It will be a good size for a fruit and vegetable garden.

See *area; metre; metric system*

hectolitre   A *hectolitre* is a metric measuring unit of volume. One *hectolitre* is equal to 100 litres.

See *litre; metric; volume*

–hedron   A word that contains the term *–hedron* refers to the faces of a solid object. *–hedron* comes from the Greek word for the face or base of a shape.

- A tetra*hedron* has four faces – 'tetra' means four. A poly*hedron* is any solid object with more than two faces – 'poly' means many.

height   The topmost point of a shape or a building is its *height*. *Height* is a measure of the distance from the bottom to the top of a shape (sometimes called the altitude of the shape). *Height* is one of the three measurements of a three-dimensional figure.

- The *height* of Table Mountain is 1 086 metres. This means that the highest point on Table Mountain is 1 086 metres above sea level.

- The *height* of a room is usually 2,6 metres.

helix   A *helix* is a spiral in three dimensions.

- A spiral staircase has the shape of a *helix*.

- The DNA molecules that contain all the instructions for how your body will develop and grow, are in the shape of a *double helix*.

See *spiral*

hemisphere   A *hemisphere* is half of a sphere. 'Hemi–' means 'half'.
- We divide the Earth into the northern *hemisphere* and the southern *hemisphere*. Iceland is in the northern hemisphere. South Africa is in the southern hemisphere.
- We could also divide the Earth into a western hemisphere and an eastern hemisphere.

See *sphere*

hepta–, heptagon, heptahedron
Hepta– comes from the Greek word for 'seven'. A *heptagon* is a polygon (a flat shape) with seven sides. A *heptahedron* is a polyhedron (a solid shape) with seven plane faces.

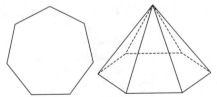

See *polygon; polyhedron*

hexa–, hexagon, hexahedron   *Hexa–* comes from the Greek word for 'six'. A *hexagon* is any polygon (a flat shape) with six straight sides. (Another name for a *hexagon* is a hexagram.)

A *hexahedron* is any polyhedron (a solid shape) with six plane faces. A regular *hexahedron* is a cube.

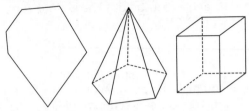

See *polygon; polyhedron*

high   A *high* object (such as a mountain) is an object whose top is far above the ground. A picture or a shelf is *high* on the wall if it is positioned near the top of the wall.
- This shelf is too *high*. The children cannot reach the books on the shelf.

See *low*

highest common factor (HCF)   The *highest common factor* is the biggest number that can divide into all the numbers in a given set of numbers without leaving any remainder. It is the biggest common divisor of all these numbers.
- In the set {32, 56, 72}:
  - the factors of 32 are: 1, 2, 4, 8, 16, 32
  - the factors of 56 are: 1, 2, 4, 7, 8, 14, 28, 56
  - the factors of 72 are: 1, 2, 4, 6, 8, 9, 12, 18, 36, 72

Therefore the *highest common factor* of the set of numbers {32, 56, 72} is 8.

See *factor*

hire purchase   *Hire purchase* is a way of buying something by paying for it over a period of months or years. You pay a deposit (a fraction of the total cost of the thing you are buying) at the start, and then you can take the item home with you. You continue to pay for it in fixed amounts (called instalments) every month until you have paid the total cost. This method of buying goods is usually more expensive than paying the total cost at the start, because the *hire purchase* price includes interest charges that you must pay every month in addition to the money that you still owe to the vendor.

- It costs R125 000 to buy this car for cash. If you buy it on *hire purchase*, you must pay a deposit of R30 000 and then pay R3 500 every month for 36 months. The total amount you will pay then is R156 000.

See *interest*

histogram   A *histogram* is a frequency diagram (bar graph) in which the area of each bar, rather than the height of each bar, gives the frequency. It is very useful when the class intervals are unequal.

- More silver cars are produced each month than any other colour car.

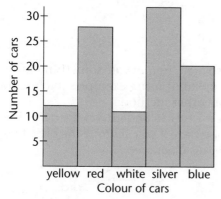

See *bar graph; frequency*

horizontal   A *horizontal* line is a line that is parallel to the horizon, or to the flat ground.

- The floor of a room is *horizontal*.

See *parallel*

horizontal arrangement   A *horizontal arrangement* is an ordering of items in a straight horizontal row, from left to right.

- Lesedi placed the pot plants in a *horizontal arrangement* in front of the house.

horizontal axis   The *horizontal axis* of a graph is the axis or line that moves from left to right across the graph, and which has the number values of the graph (the x-values) marked on it.

- The *horizontal axis* of this graph is marked in intervals of 5 mm, from 0 to 30 mm.

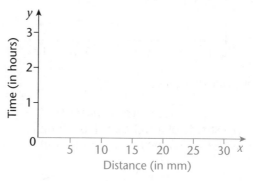

See *axis; graph*

hour   An *hour* is a unit of time measurement. 1 *hour* is equal to 60 minutes, or 3 600 seconds. There are 24 hours in 1 day.

hundredth   If a whole object is divided into one hundred equal parts, then each part of the whole is equal to one *hundredth* $\left(\frac{1}{100}\right)$.
In a long queue of people, the person who is number 100 in the queue is in the *hundredth* position.

See *fraction*

hyperbola   A *hyperbola* is a graph of points $(x; y)$ satisfying the equation $xy = k$, where k is a constant. The general form of the graph is:

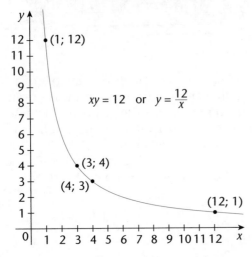

- The area of a rectangle is given by the formula $l \times b = A$. This formula is the same as the function of a *hyperbola*. To get a rectangle of area 12 cm^2, we could choose any pair of values for x and y that lies on the *hyperbola* $xy = 12$.

$$xy = 12 \quad \text{or} \quad y = \frac{12}{x}$$

See *function; graph*

hypotenuse   The *hypotenuse* is the longest side of a right-angled triangle. It is the side opposite the right angle.

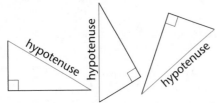

See *right angle; triangle*

icosahedron   An *icosahedron* is a polyhedron with 20 faces. A regular *icosahedron* has triangular faces; each face is an equilateral triangle. The word 'icos' comes from the Greek word for 'twenty'.

See *equilateral triangle; face; polyhedron*

identity element   An *identity element* is an element (such as a number) that can be combined with another element without changing the value of the second element. It is called an *identity element* because it allows the other element with which it combines to keep its own identity (value).

- The *identity element* for addition is 0, because when 0 is added to any number, the number does not change its value.

  $2 + 0 = 2$

  $93\ 547 + 0 = 93\ 547$

  $x + 0 = x$

  $1 + 0 = 1$

- The *identity element* for multiplication is 1, because when 1 is multiplied by any number, the number does not change its value.

  $1 \times 57 = 57$

  $1 \times a = a$

  $1 \times 0 = 0$

illustrate   To *illustrate* something means to explain it using examples, pictures or some other method.

- It is easier to understand the definition of a circle if you *illustrate* the definition with a diagram:

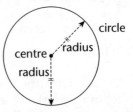

A circle is a round two-dimensional shape in which all the points on the edge (circumference) of the shape are the same distance (radius) from the centre.

image An *image* of an object (such as a shape, or a set of numbers) is what you get after you have transformed (changed) the object in some way.

- Transformation by reflection: Point P on a number line is transformed into the *image* point P' when it is reflected. A mirror reflects *images*.

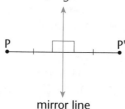

mirror line

- Transformation by enlargement: Triangle ABC is transformed when it is enlarged into the triangle *image* A'B'C'. A projector enlarges *images*.

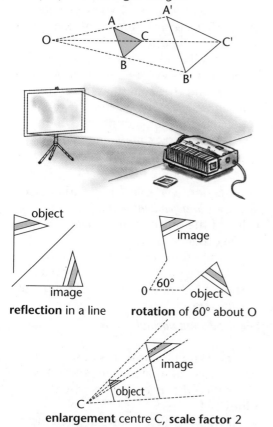

reflection in a line   **rotation** of 60° about O

enlargement centre C, **scale factor** 2

- Transformation by multiplication by 3: The set of numbers A = {0, 1, 2} is transformed to the set B = {0, 3, 6} when all the elements in A are multiplied by 3. The set B is called the *image* set of set A.

imperial units *Imperial units* are measuring units that are used in some countries, such as the United Kingdom and the USA. The word 'imperial' comes from 'empire' – it refers to the British Empire. Countries that were once colonies of Britain, such as South Africa, used *imperial units* in the past. Most of these countries have now switched over to the metric system of measuring units. (See the table on pages 151–3 of this dictionary.)

- *Imperial units* of length include the inch, foot, yard and mile.
- *Imperial units* of mass include the ounce, pound, stone and ton.
- *Imperial units* of capacity (volume) include the pint, quart and gallon.

See *metric units*

improper fraction An *improper fraction* is a fraction in which the numerator (the top number) is bigger than the denominator (the bottom number).

- Examples of *improper fractions* are:
$$\frac{6}{5}, \frac{808}{99}, \frac{378}{100}$$

See *proper fraction*

incentre, incircle The three lines that bisect (divide in half) the angles of a triangle all meet at a point inside the triangle. This point is the same distance from each side of the triangle and if you can draw a circle with its centre at this point, the circle will touch all three sides of the triangle. This point is called the *incentre*, and the circle is called the *incircle*. It is also known as an inscribed circle.

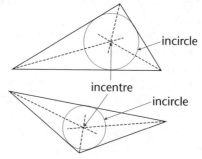

See *circle; circumcircle*

inch An *inch* is a unit of length in the imperial measuring system. It is exactly 2,54 cm long. The symbol for *inch* is ".

- You sometimes see that a size 34 dress is also labelled size 86. That is an example of centimetres and *inches* used simultaneously.

include To *include* something is to make sure that it is kept with the rest of the things you are using, showing, buying, and so on.

- Find the solution to the following equation. *Include* your working.
  $3x + 27 = 36$
  Solution:
  $$3x + 27 = 36$$
  $$3x + 27 - 27 = 36 - 27$$
  $$3x = 9$$
  $$3x \div 3 = 9 \div 3$$
  $$x = 3$$

income *Income* is money that you receive for work that you do (your wages or salary), or for goods that you sell, or for property that you rent to other people, or from bank interest, or from any other source.

- Bhekisizwe's family's *income* comes from his grandmother's pension, his mother's wage as a receptionist, and his brother's part-time job in a music store.

income tax *Income tax* is money that you pay to the government, to be used to cover the costs of things such as roads, hospitals, salaries for members of parliament, and all the other things that the government does. People who do not earn income do not pay *income tax*. People who earn under a certain amount of income every year also do not pay *income tax*.

- Lindiwe earns R12 500 per month. She pays R3 125 in *income tax* every month. This amount is deducted from her total salary by her employer before he pays her.

See *income*

incorrect Something that is *incorrect* has mistakes in it. It is wrong.

- 'Your answer is *incorrect*. You forgot to convert all the measurements to the same unit before you added them.'

increase To *increase* something means to make it bigger in size or in value.

- The maize harvest will *increase* this year because the farmers have had very good rains.
- *Increase* the price of the car by 10%:
  Car price = R105 000
  10% of R105 000 = $\frac{10}{100} \times 105\,000$
  $= R10\,500$
  Increased price = R105 000 + R10 500
  $= R115\,500$

See *decrease*

independent events Two events are *independent events* if one event does not depend on the other.

- When a die and a coin are thrown together, the events 'The die shows a three' and 'The coin shows tails' are *independent events* because the result of the coin toss does not depend on the result of the die throw (and vice versa).

See *event*

independent variable Two variables x and y are *independent variables* if the value of the one does not affect the value of the other.

- My shoe size and my hair length are *independent variables*. If my hair gets shorter or longer it does not change my shoe size.

See *dependent variable*

index When a number is raised to a power, for example 2^4, the power 4 is also called the *index*. In this case the index is 4.

- The number that follows the statement 'to the power of' is always the *index*.
  ‣ In 10^6 the *index* is 6.
  ‣ In 24^{-1} the *index* is −1.
  ‣ In 3^{55} the *index* is 55.

See *base; power*

indicate To *indicate* something means to point it out, or to show what it is, or to explain it briefly.

- Find the length of the missing side of the triangle. *Indicate* the reason for your answer.

Length of BC = 5.
Reason: BC is the hypotenuse of a right-angled triangle. Pythagoras' theorem states that $BC^2 = AB^2 + AC^2$. In this example, $BC^2 = 16 + 9 = 25$. Therefore BC = 5.

indirect proportion *Indirect proportion* is a relationship between two sets of quantities such that as the one quantity increases (gets bigger), the other quantity decreases (gets smaller).

- There is an *indirect proportion* between the number of trains available to commuters and the time it takes for people to get to work. The fewer trains there are, the longer it takes for people to get to work.

See *direct proportion; inverse proportion*

inequality An *inequality* is a mathematical statement that relates two things (such as number values) by saying that one thing is 'greater than', 'less than', 'greater than or equal to' or 'less than or equal to' the other thing. The symbols for these inequalities are:

> 'greater than' : $a > b$ means 'a is greater than b'.
< 'less than': $a < b$ means 'a is less than b'.
≥ 'greater than or equal to': $a \geq b$ means 'a is greater than or equal to b'.
≤ 'less than or equal to': $a \leq b$ means 'a is less than or equal to b'.

- All these statements are *inequalities*:
  $12 < 13$
  $200 > 20$
  $a + 1 > 1$ if a is a positive integer
  $b - 1 \leq -2$ if b is a negative integer

See *equal*

infinite set An *infinite set* of numbers is a set that goes on forever, with no 'last number'. We write an *infinite set* by using three dots to show that we could keep adding more numbers to the set, like this: A = {1, 2, 3, ...}

- The set of powers of 2 is an *infinite set*:
  P = {2, 4, 8, 16, 32, ...}
- The set of negative integers is an *infinite set*:
  I = {−1, −2, −3, −4, −5, ...}

See *finite*

infinity *Infinity* is the imaginary place you would get to if you could reach the end of an infinite set or infinite thing. You can never really get to *infinity* because if you could, then it would be a definite point at the end of a set of things, which means it would be part of a finite set. The symbol for *infinity* is ∞.

inscribe To *inscribe* means to draw one shape inside another shape. When one shape fits inside another shape it is called an *inscribed* shape.

- A circle can be *inscribed* inside a triangle to touch all three sides of the triangle.

- A square can be *inscribed* inside a circle so that its four vertices (corners) all touch the circle's circumference.

insert To *insert* something means to fit it into something else, in a particular position.

- *Insert* the screws into the holes at the four corners of the plank.
- *Insert* the correct arithmetic sign into this number sentence: 3 ☐ 12 = 36
  Answer: 3 ☒ 12 = 36

inside (space and position)　The *inside* of a container is the space within the walls of the container.

The *inside* of an object is its inner surface, that part that you cannot see from outside.

- Sandy keeps her books *inside* her wardrobe to protect them from her baby brother.

See *outside*

instalment　An *instalment* is a fixed part of the total amount of money that you must pay for something you buy. *Instalments* are usually paid every week or every month until the full amount has been repaid.

- Suresh bought a motorbike for R25 000. He is paying for it in *instalments* of R750 every month. It will take him nearly three years to pay for the bike.

See *hire purchase*

insurance　*Insurance* is a kind of financial protection that you can buy to get back the value of your possessions if they are destroyed in a fire or flood, or if someone steals them. You pay an amount of money every month for this protection, and if you lose the things you have insured, the insurance company gives you enough money to buy new ones.

- 'My roof was destroyed in the storm. Luckily I have *insurance* on my house, so the *insurance* company will pay for the cost of replacing the roof.'

integer　An *integer* is any positive or negative whole number, or zero. The set of *integers* is infinite.

- Positive and negative *integers* can be shown on a number line:

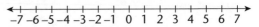

See *whole number*

intercept　An *intercept* is the point on a graph where the graph cuts the *x*-axis or the *y*-axis of the Cartesian plane. A graph can have more than one *intercept*, depending on its shape.

- This graph has two *intercepts*.

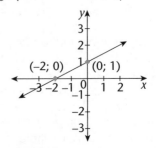

- This parabola has three *intercepts*.

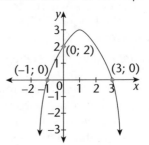

See *axis; graph*

interest　*Interest* is an amount of money that is added to money you are saving or borrowing. If you save money in a bank account, the bank pays you *interest* at a fixed percentage of your savings. If you borrow money from the bank, you must pay *interest* to the bank as a 'fee' for being allowed to use the bank's money.

- Sarah kept R2 000 in a savings account for five years. At the end of that time she had R2 700 in the account. The R700 was *interest* that her savings had earned.

See *compound interest; simple interest*

interior angle　An *interior angle* of a polygon is an angle formed inside the polygon at a vertex (a point where two sides of the polygon meet).

- A triangle has 3 *interior angles*.

- A quadrilateral has 4 *interior angles*.

- A hexagon has 6 *interior angles*.

See *exterior angle*

interpolate　To *interpolate* means to estimate a value between two number values that you already know.

- Laura's height on 1 January last year was 1,52 m. On 1 January this year her height was 1,56 m. We can *interpolate* that her height halfway through last year was 1,54 m – this would be a reasonable estimate.

See *extrapolate*

interquartile range　The *interquartile range* is a measure of spread of a set of statistical data. It is the difference between the lower quartile and the upper quartile.

See *data; quartile*

intersect　When two or more lines or curves cross each other, they *intersect*.

- Lines AB and CD *intersect* at E.

- The line FG *intersects* the circle at K and L.

- Line ST *intersects* line GH at Y and line MN at Z.

intersection of sets　The *intersection of two (or more) sets* is the set of elements that are common to both (or all) the sets. The symbol for *intersection of sets* is ∩. On a Venn diagram, the area where the sets overlap is the *intersection of* the *sets*.

- If A = {3, 4, 5, 6, 7, 8} and B = {4, 6, 8, 10, 12} then A ∩ B = {4, 6, 8}.

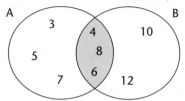

See *element of a set; Venn diagram*

interval　An *interval* is a set of numbers between a given starting number and end number. You can specify what kinds of numbers are included in the *interval*, and what its start and end points are.

- The *interval* of real numbers from 2 to 3 inclusive contains all real numbers between 2 and 3, and includes 2 and 3. It can be expressed as: $2 \leq x \leq 3$.

- The *interval* of real numbers from 2 to 3 exclusive contains all real numbers between 2 and 3, but excludes 2 and 3. It can be expressed as $2 < x < 3$.

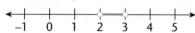

See *real number*

invariant　An *invariant* is a property that stays the same during a transformation. For example, when a triangle is transformed by enlargement, the angles stay the same but the lengths of the sides change. So the angles are *invariant* in the transformation.

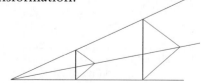

See *transformation*

inverse operation　An *inverse operation* is a mathematical operation that has the opposite effect to another operation. If you perform an operation on a number, and then perform the *inverse operation* on your answer, you will obtain the original number that you started with.

- Subtraction is the *inverse operation* of addition. Addition is the *inverse operation* of subtraction.

$$3 + 5 = 8 \qquad 8 - 5 = 3$$

- Adding 5 is the inverse operation to substracting 5.
- Multiplication is the *inverse operation* of division.

$$12 \times 5 = 60 \qquad 60 \div 5 = 12$$

- Squaring a number is the *inverse operation* of finding the square root of a number.

$$4^2 = 16 \qquad \sqrt{16} = 4$$

inverse proportion, inversely proportional　Two quantities are *inversely proportional* if the one decreases (gets smaller) as the other one increases (gets bigger).

- Speed and time are *inversely proportional*. The faster you travel, the less time it takes you to get to your destination. So as your speed increases the time of your journey decreases. If you travel at 20 km/h it will take you approximately 5 hours to get to a destination that is 100 km away. If you travelled at 100 km/h it would take you about 1 hour to get there.

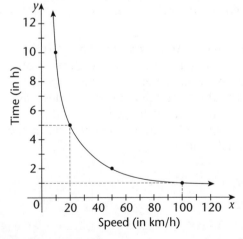

See *direct proportion*

invert　To *invert* something means to turn it upside down, or to reverse the order or position or relationship of two or more things.

- If you *invert* the symbol for the number 6 you get the symbol for the number 9.
- If you *invert* the proper fraction $\frac{3}{4}$ you get an improper fraction $\frac{4}{3}$.
- Many patterns consist of a shape that is combined with an *inverted* form of the same shape.

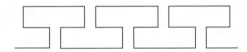

invest, investment　To *invest* money means to place the money in a bank, to buy shares in a business, or to do something else with the money that will earn more money in the future. An *investment* plan is a plan for making sure that you will have more money in the future than you have now.

- Some people believe it is a good idea to *invest* money by buying property such as land or houses, because the value of property *investments* usually increases over time.

investigation　An *investigation* is a process of analysing a problem to find ways of solving it. In an investigation, you study the facts that you know about the problem, and you test out different methods of finding the answer until you see which method works.

irrational number   An *irrational number* is a number that cannot be written in the form of a rational number – that is, as one number divided by another number, $\frac{a}{b}$, where *a* and *b* are positive or negative whole numbers.

- Some examples of *irrational numbers* are π, $\sqrt{2}$, $\sqrt{3}$. None of these numbers can be written in the form $\frac{a}{b}$, because their decimal portions are not terminating or recurring decimals.

See *rational number; recurring decimal; terminating decimal; whole number*

isometric paper   *Isometric paper* is paper that is covered with a grid of equilateral triangles. It is useful for illustrating three-dimensional objects.

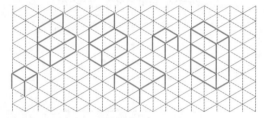

See *equilateral triangle*

isometry   The word *isometry* means 'equal measure'. An *isometry* is a transformation in which the distance between any two points is unchanged by the transformation. Rotations, reflections and translations are *isometries* because they do not change the distance between points on the shape. Enlargements are not *isometries* because they change the lengths between points on a shape.

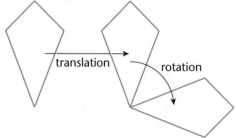

See *transformation*

isosceles triangle (pronounced: i-so'-se-leese)   An *isosceles triangle* is a triangle that has two sides of equal length and two equal angles opposite the equal sides.

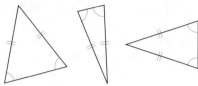

See *triangle*

item   An *item* is a general word that we use to refer to a separate thing in a group of things. It can be used for concrete things such as food, books and clothes or for abstract things such as questions, problems, numbers and shapes.

- There are three *items* of clothing in his shopping trolley: a pair of shoes, a jacket and a scarf.
- Group the *items* below into two-dimensional shapes and three-dimensional objects:

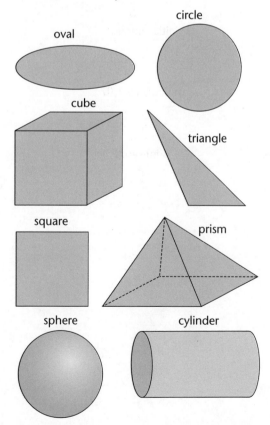

iterative procedure   The word 'reiterate' means 'to say again'. In mathematics an *iterative procedure* is a repetitive process – you apply the same method again and again to get the solution to a problem.

- A calculator can be used to find how a sum of money, for example R1 000, grows when it earns 7% interest per year. To do this, you enter 1 000 into the calculator and then repeatedly multiply by 1,07:

Sum invested: R1 000,00
Amount at end of year 1:
1 000 × 1,07 = R1 070,00
Amount at end of year 2:
1 070 × 1,07 = R1 144,90
Amount at end of year 3:
1 144,90 × 1,07 = R1 225,043

This is an *iterative procedure*. The general rule for this procedure can be expressed in an algebraic form:

The amount Ra_n, at the end of year n, and the amount Ra_{n+1} at the end of year $n + 1$, are connected by the iterative relation $a_{n+1} = 1,07a_n$.

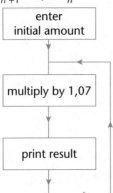

J

join   To *join* means to become part of something. To *join* two or more things means to put them together to form one (bigger) thing.

- If you *join* two semi-circles you get a full circle.

- If you *join* two points, you get a line segment.

- If you *join* all the points you have plotted on this graph, you get a parabola.

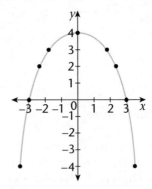

justify   To *justify* something means to give reasons that prove it is true.

- When you give the answer to a calculation, you can *justify* your answer by explaining all the steps you used in the calculation.

K

L

kilogram A *kilogram* is a unit for measuring mass in the metric system. 1 *kilogram* is equal to 1 000 grams. 'Kilo-' means 'one thousand'. The abbreviation of *kilogram* is kg.

See *gram; metric system*

kilolitre A *kilolitre* is a unit for measuring volume (capacity) in the metric system. 1 *kilolitre* is equal to 1 000 litres. 'Kilo-' means 'one thousand'. The abbreviation of *kilolitre* is kl.

See *litre; metric system*

kilometre A *kilometre* is a unit for measuring distance in the metric system. 1 *kilometre* is equal to 1 000 metres. 'Kilo-' means 'one thousand'. The abbreviation of *kilometre* is km.

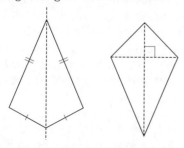

See *metre; metric system*

kite A *kite* is a quadrilateral with two pairs of equal and adjacent sides and one line of symmetry. The diagonals of a *kite* are at right angles to each other.

See *line of symmetry; quadrilateral; right angle*

large 1. A *large* shape or object is a shape or object that is big.
2. A *large* number is a number with a high value.
- The *large* triangle in this group is ∆PQR. All the small triangles can fit inside this *large* triangle.

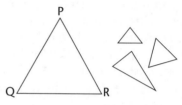

- A *large* number of people will go to the World Cup football final match – eighty thousand people can fit inside the stadium.

last The *last* item in a group is the item at the end or back of the group. The *last* event (happening) in a group of events is the one that happens after all the other events have happened.
- Lydia is the *last* person in the queue. There are four people standing ahead of her.
- The last bus leaves the city at 20:10 every weeknight.

See *first*

latitude *Latitudes* are imaginary lines around the Earth's surface, parallel to the Equator. Each line of *latitude* forms a circle whose centre is on the imaginary line that joins the North and South Poles. They are named using angle degrees north or south of the Equator. We draw lines of *latitude* on maps, and use them to describe the position of places on Earth. They are sometimes also called parallels of *latitude*.
- Cape Town and Port Elizabeth lie very close to the line of *latitude* at 34° south of the Equator. Ulundi lies close to the line of *latitude* at 28° south of the Equator.

See *longitude*

law   A *law* in mathematics is a rule or method that you must always use for solving a certain kind of problem.

- The *laws* of indices tell you how to do calculations with index numbers (powers) in an expression. For example, they say that $a^2 \times a^5 = a^{2+5} = a^7$.

leap year   A normal year has 365 days. A *leap year* is a year with one extra day – 366 days. This day is always placed at the end of February – the date is 29 February. A *leap year* happens once every 4 years.

- Someone who is born on 29 February will only have a 'real' birthday once every four years!

least expensive   The *least expensive* item is the item that costs the least amount of money.

- Sibusiso chose the *least expensive* pair of trainers in the shop. His mother was very happy about this.

left   The *left* side of an object is the side that is towards the west if the object is facing north.

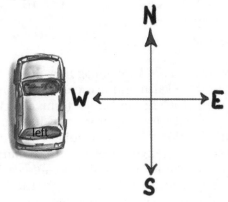

See *right*

length   The *length* of an object is how much it measures from one end to the other end along the longest side of the object. *Length* is usually measured in the metric units millimetres, centimetres, metres or kilometres.

- The *length* of this field is 90 metres.

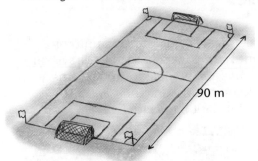

90 m

See *metric system*

less   One number is *less* than another number if it is smaller than that number.

- Thembisa gets *less* pocket money than Thoko because she is younger than Thoko.

letter   A *letter* is a symbol that represents one of the sounds in the alphabet. In algebra we use *letter* symbols as well as number symbols.

- There are 26 *letters* in our alphabet: a b c d e f g h i j k l m n o p q r s t u v w x y z
- There are 24 *letters* in the Greek alphabet: α β γ δ ε ζ η θ ι κ λ μ ν ξ ο π ρ σ τ υ φ χ ψ ω

See *algebra*

light (mass)   A *light* object is an object that is easy to lift or carry because its mass is so low.

- A feather is very *light*. It takes longer to fall to the ground than a stone, which is much heavier.

See *heavy*

limit   A sequence of numbers has a *limit* L. If the numbers get closer and closer to L as the sequence proceeds, the difference between the numbers and L gets closer and closer to 0. (Note that the *limit* L itself can be any number – it need not be 0.)

- The sequence 2,9; 2,99; 2,999; ... gets closer and closer to 3 – that is, its *limit* is 3. The difference between any term in the sequence and the *limit* 3 gets smaller and smaller – that is, it gets closer and closer to 0.

line A *line* extends indefinitely in two directions – that is, it goes on forever to the left and to the right. This is sometimes shown by dashes at each end of the *line*, or by arrowheads at each end.

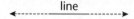
line

See *line segment*

linear, linear graph, linear relation
Something is *linear* if it is in the shape of a line, or relates to a line in some way. A *linear graph* has the shape of a straight line.

- The graph shows a *linear relation* between the number of dollars (x) and the number of rands (y). $y = 7,5x$

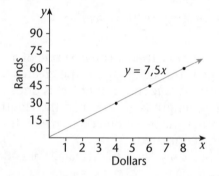

This means that each \$1 = R7,50. If you plot the points for different values of x and join the points, you will get a straight line.

See *relation*

linear equation A *linear equation* is an equation with variables of degree to the power of 1. The graph of a *linear equation* is a straight line.

- These are all *linear equations*:
  $2x + 3y = 4$
  $x + 2 = 0$
  $5x + 2y - 3z = 1$
  The power of every variable in these equations is 1. (Remember that if a number or variable has the power 1, we usually do not write in the power: $x^1 = x$.)

See *linear, linear graph, linear relation*

linear scale factor If an object or a shape is enlarged so that the lengths of all the lines are multiplied by the same number k, then k is called the *linear scale factor* of the enlargement.

- In the diagram, the lengths of all the lines in the small shape have been multiplied by 2 to enlarge the shape. The *linear scale factor* of the enlargement is 2.

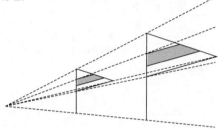

See *similar figures*

line graph A *line graph* is a graph in which separate points plotted on the graph are joined by straight lines.

- The temperatures at different times of the day have been plotted as points on this graph. The points are joined to form a *line graph*. This *line graph* shows how the temperature goes up and down over time.

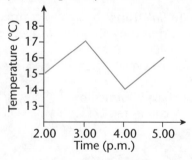

line of symmetry A *line of symmetry* is a line that can be drawn through a two-dimensional shape so that the parts of the shape on each side of the line are exactly the same shape. If a shape has line symmetry it means that there is a *line of symmetry*.

- This shape has 1 *line of symmetry*.

- This shape has 2 *lines of symmetry*.

rectangle

- This shape has 4 *lines of symmetry*.

square

- This shape has no *lines of symmetry*.

parallelogram

See *reflection; symmetry*

line segment   A *line segment* is a part of a line between any two fixed points on the line.

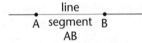

line segment AB

See *line*

link   To *link* things means to connect them so that they are joined together.
- The children *link* hands to form a circle.

- This chain is formed by many connected *links*.

liquid   A *liquid* is a substance that does not have a fixed shape, but flows easily from one container to another and fits the shape of any container.
- The woman pours the tea from the pot into the cups.

See *solid*

list   A *list* is a group of words, numbers or symbols, written one after the other, in any order that makes sense.
- Shopping *list*: sugar butter eggs tea coffee jam tomatoes flour …
- *List* of class results: Linda 75% Pumezo 81% George 69% Anna 77% …

litre   A *litre* is a metric unit for measuring the capacity of a container or the volume of liquid in the container. 1 *litre* is equal to 1 000 millilitres. The abbreviation for *litre* is ℓ.

See *capacity; metric system*

long, longer than   The *long* side of a shape is the side that has the greater length. A *long* shape or object is one whose length is greater than the length of other shapes or objects to which it is being compared.
- The *long* sides of this rectangle are AB and CD.

- The road from Cape Town to Johannesburg that goes through Kimberley is *longer than* the road that goes through Bloemfontein.

See *short*

long division   *Long division* is a method for doing division calculations using several steps.
- $288 \div 4$
  Method 1
  (Decompose – breaking up)
  $= (200 \div 4) + (80 \div 4) + (8 \div 4)$
  $= 50 + 20 + 2$
  $= 72$

Method 2
(Subtract many times)

$25 + 25 + 22 = 72$

```
4 )288
  -100   (25 × 4)
   188
  -100   (25 × 4)
    88
   -88   (22 × 4)
  ─────
         (72 × 4)
```

Method 3
(Halving)

$288 ÷ 4 \quad (4 = 2 × 2)$
$= (288 ÷ 2) ÷ 2$
$= 144 ÷ 2$
$= 72$

Method 4
(Subtracting by multiplying)

```
     ·72
 4 )288   (4 cannot go into 2 – add the 8)
  - 28↓   (7 × 4) (subtract first)
   ··8    (bring down the 8)
   - 8    (4 × 2)
    ·
```

long hand The *long hand* or minute hand on a clock face shows the number of minutes that have passed.

See *clock face; short hand*

longitude Lines of *longitude* are imaginary lines around the surface of the Earth that pass through the North and South Poles. They are used to fix the positions of places on Earth. Their positions are described using angle degrees. The line of *longitude* that passes through Greenwich, a town in England, is given the angle 0° and called the Greenwich meridian. The angle positions of the other lines of *longitude* are measured from the Greenwich meridian.

• The line of *longitude* that is 20° east of the Greenwich meridian passes through South Africa. Cape Town is very close to this line, and the *longitude* of Cape Town

is about 18°E. The city of Chennai in India is 80°E. New York is 74°W.

• Lines of *longitude* are used to divide the world into different time zones. All the places between the same two lines of *longitude* will be in the same time zone, which means they will have the same time of day.

See *latitude; meridian*

long multiplication *Long multiplication* is a method for doing multiplication calculations using several steps.

• **Method 1**

$28 × 24$
$= (20 + 8) × 24$
$= (20 × 24) + (8 × 24)$
$= 480 + 8 × (20 + 4)$
$= 480 + 160 + 32$
$= 672$

Method 2

$28 × 24$
$= (10 + 10 + 2 + 2 + 2 + 2) × 24$
$= 240 + 240 + 48 + 48 + 48 + 48$
$= 480 + 192$
$= 672$

Method 3

$28 × 24$
$= 14 × 48 \quad$ *Halve 28, double 24.*
$= 7 × 96 \quad$ *Halve 14, double 48.*
$= 7 × (90 + 6)$
$= 630 + 42$
$= 672$

Method 4

```
     28
   ×  24
  ─────
    112   (28 × 4)
  + 560   (28 × 20)
  ─────
    672
```

loss, percentage loss   A *loss* is an amount of money or an object that you have lost. In business, if the goods in the shop cost the shopkeeper more money than they can be sold for, the shop makes a *loss*. The *percentage loss* is the percentage of the total cost that you have lost.

- Mrs Mtimkulu spent R3 000 on new CDs to sell in her shop. But all the CDs were scratched, so she had to sell them at a discount – she only earned R1 000 from the sales. She made a *loss* of R2 000 on these CDs. She worked out that her *percentage loss* was $\frac{2\ 000}{3\ 000} \times \frac{100}{1} = 66,7\%$.

See *profit*

low   1. A *low* amount is an amount that is smaller than normal.
2. A *low* position is a position close to the bottom level.

- 'The prices in that shop are *low*! I expected to pay much more for these jeans.'
- In the children's room, the bookshelf is *low*, so that the children can reach the books by themselves.

See *high*

lowest common multiple (LCM)   The *lowest common multiple* of two numbers is the smallest number that is a multiple of both numbers. The *lowest common multiple* of three or more numbers is the smallest number that is a multiple of all these numbers.

- The multiples of 6 are: 6, 12, 18, 24, 30, 36, ...
- The multiples of 15 are: 15, 30, 45, 60, ...
- The *lowest common multiple (LCM)* of 6 and 15 is 30. There are many other common multiples of 6 and 15 but they are all higher numbers than 30.

See *common multiple*

lowest terms   A fraction is in its *lowest terms* if there are no common factors that can be divided into the numerator and the denominator. This is another way of saying that the fraction is in its simplest form.

- To write the fraction $\frac{25}{30}$ in its *lowest terms*, we divide the numerator and the denominator by their highest common factor, which is 5:
$$\frac{25}{30} \div \frac{5}{5} = \frac{5}{6}$$

See *common factor; fraction*

M

magic square A *magic square* is an arrangement of numbers in a square so that each of the rows, columns and diagonals adds up to the same total. Often the numbers 1 to 9 or 1 to 16 are used, but other sets of numbers can be used.

8	1	6
3	5	7
4	9	2

8 + 1 + 6 = 15
8 + 3 + 4 = 15
8 + 5 + 2 = 15

Magic total = 15

16	2	3	13
5	11	10	8
9	7	6	12
4	14	15	1

Magic total = 34

5	12	7
10	8	6
9	4	11

Magic total = 24

magnitude The *magnitude* of a number is its size (how big it is). We ignore its sign (whether it is positive or negative).
- The *magnitude* of –2 is 2 and the *magnitude* of +2 is also 2. Both –2 and +2 take up 2 units on the number line.

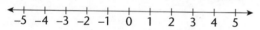

major arc Two points A and B on a circle, not at the ends of a diameter, divide the circumference into two arcs. The larger of these two arcs is called the *major arc*.

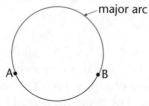

See *arc of a circle; circumference; diameter; minor arc*

major sector See *sector of a circle*

major segment If a line segment is divided into two unequal parts, the *major segment* is the part that is longer.
- On the line segment AB, AC is the *major segment*.

A　　major segment　　　C　　　　B

See *minor segment*

manipulate To *manipulate* something means to make it work by moving its parts correctly.
- Thembeka knows how to make the kite fly by *manipulating* the string as the wind blows.

many *Many* means 'a lot' or a large number of things.
- There are *many* grains in even a small handful of sand – too many to count!

See *few*

mapping *Mapping* is another name for a mathematical function. It comes from the geographical idea of making a map in which there is one unique point on the map for each point on the ground. A function is a mathematical relation in which there is only one value of the variable y for each value of the variable x. We can say that each value of x 'maps onto' one value of y.
- In the mathematical function $y = x + 1$, x is any positive or negative integer on the number line. This *mapping* diagram shows the value of y that we get for each value of x.

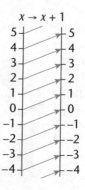

$x \rightarrow x + 1$

See *function*

mark To *mark* something is to make a sign on it to show that you have noticed it, or counted it, or chosen it.

- Make a *mark* next to your favourite food.

- *Mark* the numbers in this list that are multiples of 5.

2, 3, ⑮, ⑥⓪, 72, ⑦⑤, 87, ⑨⓪

mark off To *mark off* certain values means to make marks on a line, a graph or another shape to show the position of each value.

- The horizontal and vertical axes of this graph are *marked off* in units of 5 mm:

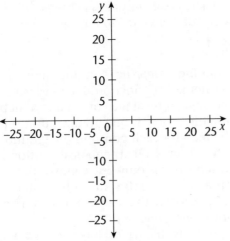

- A point Z, 3 cm from C, is *marked off* on the line segment CD:

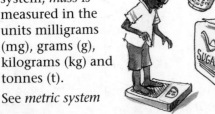

mass The *mass* of an object is the amount of matter in it. In the metric system, *mass* is measured in the units milligrams (mg), grams (g), kilograms (kg) and tonnes (t).

See *metric system*

match To *match* things means to find the things that belong together.

- *Match* these objects to the correct containers:

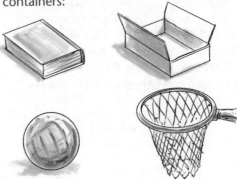

mathematical accuracy *Mathematical accuracy* is an expression that is used to indicate that something is planned and measured very precisely.

- When a building is constructed, the engineers and builders have to plan the size and shape of the building with *mathematical accuracy*, otherwise the building may be unstable and could collapse.

mathematical instruments *Mathematical instruments* are tools that are used to construct accurate shapes, measure quantities and calculate values, using mathematical methods.

- These are examples of *mathematical instruments*:

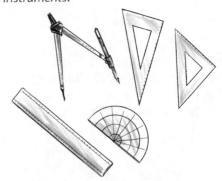

mathematical modelling *Mathematical modelling* is a way of using mathematics to analyse a complex problem, and find a solution. The problem is simplified by ignoring some of its parts, and mathematical methods are used to solve the simplified problem. This simplified solution is then tested on the real problem to see whether it helps to solve the problem.

mathematician   A *mathematician* is someone who investigates the properties of numbers, shapes and spaces using mathematical methods, and who invents new mathematical concepts and methods.

mathematics   *Mathematics* is the science that studies the properties of quantities, shapes and space, and the ways in which these properties can be applied to solve practical problems. Arithmetic, geometry, algebra, trigonometry and calculus are some of the sets of concepts and methods that make up *mathematics*.
- Princess Nefertiabet's scribes in Giza, Ancient Egypt, would have written 1996 like this:

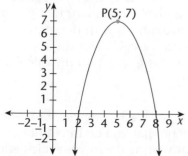

| 1 × 1 000 | 9 × 100 | 9 × 10 | 6 × 1 |

- In the Paleolithic era (about 15 000 BCE), traders would notch a reindeer's antler to record clients' buying on credit. Clients kept a similar record. Cheating was impossible because you couldn't remove notches from the hard antler.

maximum   *Maximum* means 'highest amount'. The *maximum* of a function can refer to the turning point on a graph, or to the *y*-coordinate of this point.
- The *maximum* percentage that you can get for your test result is 100%.
- The *maximum* of this quadratic function is the point P(5; 7).

See *minimum*

mean   A *mean* is one type of average value used in statistics. An average is a measure of the most common events in a group of statistical data. To calculate the *mean*, you add all the data together and divide the total by the number of data events in the group.
- In a class test, 9 learners got the following marks:
  6, 5, 8, 12, 3, 5, 7, 7, 5
  The *mean* mark for this group of learners is therefore:
  $(6 + 5 + 8 + 12 + 3 + 5 + 7 + 7 + 5) \div 9$
  $= 58 \div 9 = 6{,}44$

See *average; event; median; mode*

measure   To *measure* something means to find the size of one or more of its features – such as its length, breadth, height, capacity, mass.

See *measurement*

measurement   A *measurement* is a number value that describes the size of a shape or object.
- These are examples of different types of *measurement*:
  › Light travels at a speed of 186 000 km/s.
  › The tallest man in the world has a height of 2,7 m.
  › When this baby was born, her mass was only 1,5 kg.
  › The deepest part of the sea bed is in the Pacific Ocean – it is 10 918 m (nearly 11 km) below sea level.

See *depth; height; mass; speed*

measures of central tendency   *Measures of central tendency* are ways of measuring how often certain data events occur. There are three *measures of central tendency* that we commonly use in statistical analysis: the mean, the median and the mode.
- The buyers for clothing shops use *measures of central tendency* to work out what clothing sizes customers buy most often.

See *data; event; mean; median; mode*

measures of dispersion

Measures of dispersion are ways of measuring how widely data events are spread out around the average value.

- Most learners in the school get year-marks of between 40% and 60%, so the class average mark is in this range. But there are also learners who get marks as low as 10% and as high as 85%. The principal uses *measures of dispersion* to find out the complete range of all the learners' results.

See *average*

median

A *median* is one type of average value used in statistics. An average is a measure of the most common events in a group of statistical data. To find the *median*, you arrange the data events in the group in order of their size, smallest to largest. The *median* is the middle event (value) in this new arrangement.

- In a class test, 9 learners got the following marks:
  6, 5, 8, 12, 3, 5, 7, 7, 5
  To find the *median*, first rearrange the marks in order of their size:
  3, 5, 5, 5, 6, 7, 7, 8, 12
  The *median* is the middle number in this arrangement, which is 6.
- If there were an even number of data events in the group, there would not be one middle event. In that case the

median is calculated as the mean of the two middle scores.

For example, there are six events in the following groups of marks:
10, 12, 9, 19, 7, 11
To get the *median*, first arrange the events in order of size:
7, 9, 10, 11, 12, 19
Now calculate the mean of the two middle numbers 10 and 11:
$(10 + 11) \div 2 = 10,5$. This is the *median* of the data.

See *average; event; mean; mode*

median of a triangle

A *median of a triangle* is a line that joins one vertex of the triangle to the midpoint of the opposite side. A triangle has three medians, one from each vertex. The three medians always meet at one point, called the centroid.

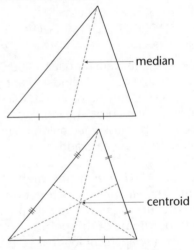

See *midpoint; vertex*

memory key

The *memory key* is a key (button) on the calculator that you use to do calculations with the number shown on the calculator display and the number that is stored in the calculator's memory.

mental arithmetic

Mental arithmetic is arithmetic that you do in your head, without writing down your calculations. 'Mental' means 'of the mind'.

- Anne can use *mental arithmetic* to add up the prices of all the things she buys at the supermarket. At the tillpoint she checks to see whether she calculated the same total as the cashier gets on her till.

menu (computer)   A *menu* is a list of options (choices) that you see on a computer screen when you are using a computer program. The *menu* usually 'drops down' from a bar at the top of the screen.

meridian   A *meridian* is an imaginary line around Earth that passes through the North and South Poles. *Meridians* are known as lines of longitude.
- The Greenwich *meridian* is the *meridian* that passes through the town of Greenwich, in England. The positions of the lines of longitude around the world are defined by saying that the Greenwich *meridian* is at the position 0°. The angles of all the other lines of longitude are measured from this position.

See *longitude*

method   A *method* is a step-by-step way of doing something such as solving a problem, constructing an object or calculating an answer, in which you always use the same steps in the same order, to get the correct result.
- In mathematics there are *methods* for many different kinds of task, for example:
  ‣ the *method* for doing long division
  ‣ the *method* for constructing a perpendicular bisector on a line segment
  ‣ the *method* for calculating the volume of a cuboid.

metre   A *metre* is a unit of length in the metric system of measurement. The people who created the metric system decided that a certain length would be called one *metre*, and all other length

measurements would be calculated in relation to this basic unit:

1 km = 1 000 m

$1 \text{ cm} = \frac{1}{100} \text{ m}$

$1 \text{ mm} = \frac{1}{1\,000} \text{ m}.$

See *metric system*

metre stick   A *metre stick* is a rod or a ruler exactly 1 m long, used for measuring metre lengths.
See *metre*

metre wheel   A *metre wheel* is a tool that is used to measure long distances. As the wheel rolls along the ground, it measures the distance it has moved and this is shown in metre units on the wheel.

metric system, metric units   The *metric system* is a system of measurement that is based on measuring units calculated in multiples of 10, such as tens, hundreds, thousands, tenths, hundredths and thousandths. These are called *metric units*. Most countries in the world use the *metric system* for all their standard measurements.
- The *metric units* that are most commonly used in the *metric system* can be seen in the table on pages 151–3 of this dictionary.

micron   A *micron* is a measuring unit for very tiny lengths. 1 *micron* is equal to 1 millionth of a metre. Another name for a *micron* is a micrometre. The symbol for a *micron* is μm.
- The diameter of a human hair is about 70 *microns* (70 μm).

midday   *Midday* is 12 o'clock at noon, which we think of as the 'middle' of the day. Before *midday* it is morning; after *midday* it is afternoon. *Midday* is 12 hours after midnight.

See *midnight; noon*

middle   1. The *middle* position is the position exactly equal distances (half-way) between two given end points.
2. The *middle* item in a group of items is the item that has the same number of items before it and after it.

- The line segment AB is 5 cm long. The point M is exactly in the *middle* of AB, because AM = 2,5 cm and MB = 2,5 cm.

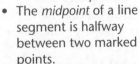

- There are 7 floors in Zanele's block of flats. Zanele's family lives on the *middle* floor, which is the 4th floor up from the ground.
- In the set of elements:
  Z = {388, 4, 19, 276, 55, 100, 12, 76, 900}
  the *middle* element is 55.

See *midpoint*

midnight   *Midnight* is 12 o'clock at night, which we think of as the 'middle' of the night. Before *midnight* it is late evening or night; after *midnight* it is very early morning. *Midnight* is 12 hours after midday.

See *midday; noon*

midpoint   A *midpoint* is a point exactly halfway between two other points.

- The *midpoint* of a circle is the centre of the circle. All the points on the circumference of the circle are the same distance from the *midpoint*.
- The *midpoint* of a line segment is halfway between two marked points.

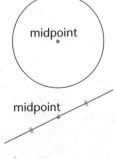

See *centre of a circle; middle*

mile   A *mile* is a measuring unit of distance in the imperial system. 1 *mile* is equal to 1 760 yards, which is 5 280 feet (1 yard = 3 feet). To convert *miles* to kilometres we say that 5 *miles* are approximately equal to 8 kilometres, or 1 kilometre $\approx \frac{5}{8}$ *mile*.

- In South Africa, *miles* were used to measure distances until about 1970. Old maps and atlases sometimes show the distances between cities in *miles*. The *mile* is still used in the United Kingdom, the USA, and in international aviation.

See *imperial units; kilometre*

millennium   A *millennium* is a period of one thousand years.

- 31 December 2000 was the end of the second *millennium* in the calendar that we use. Many countries celebrated this event with big parties.

See *century; decade*

millilitre   A *millilitre* is a measure of volume in the metric system. 1 *millilitre* is equal to $\frac{1}{1\,000}$ litre. It is the same as a cubic centimetre. The abbreviation for *millilitres* is ml.

- A medicine spoon usually holds 5 ml of liquid. In recipes, a teaspoon usually holds 5 ml and a tablespoon holds 15 ml of liquid.

See *litre; metric system; tablespoon; teaspoon*

millimetre   A *millimetre* is a measure of length in the metric system. 1 *millimetre* is equal to $\frac{1}{1\,000}$ metre. The abbreviation for *millimetres* is mm.

- The markings between the centimetre marks on a ruler show *millimetres*. There are 10 mm in 1 cm.

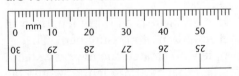

See *centimetre; metre; metric system*

million   A *million* is 10 multiplied by itself 6 times, or 10^6. It is written as 1 000 000. In the base 10 number system, the *millions* place is the 7th place to the left of the decimal comma.

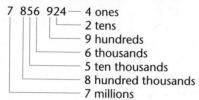

7 856 924 — 4 ones
— 2 tens
— 9 hundreds
— 6 thousands
— 5 ten thousands
— 8 hundred thousands
— 7 millions

See *base of a number*

minimum   *Minimum* means 'lowest amount'. The *minimum* of a function can refer to its turning point or the *y*-value at this point.
- The *minimum* percentage that you can get for your test result is 0%.
- The *minimum* of this quadratic function is the point P(2; –6).

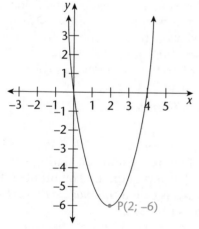

See *maximum*

minor arc   Two points A and B on a circle, not at the ends of a diameter, divide the circumference into two arcs. The smaller of these two arcs is called the *minor arc*.

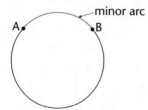

See *arc of a circle; circumference; diameter; major arc*

minor sector   See *sector of a circle*

minor segment   If a line segment is divided into two unequal parts, the *minor segment* is the part that is shorter.
- On the line segment AB, CB is the *minor segment*.

See *major segment*

minus   The *minus* symbol is the symbol '–' which means 'subtract'. We sometimes say 'A minus B' to mean 'subtract B from A'.
- 200 – 70 = 130
  Two hundred *minus* seventy equals one hundred and thirty.

minute (angles)   A *minute* is a unit for measuring angles to a high level of accuracy. We usually use degrees to measure angles, but to be more precise, we could measure the exact number of *minutes* between two degrees. There are 60 *minutes* in 1 degree. The symbol for *minute* units is '.
- The exact size of this angle is 70° 42'.

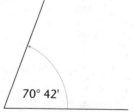

70° 42'

- The angle exactly halfway between 30° and 35° is the angle at 32° 30'.

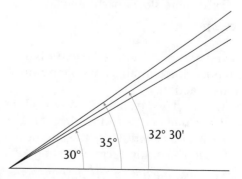

30°　　35°　　32° 30'

See *degree*

minute (time)　A *minute* is a unit for measuring time. There are 60 *minutes* in 1 hour. One *minute* is 60 seconds long.

- The school day lasts for about 6 hours, which means you spend 360 *minutes* at school every day.

See *hour; second (unit of time)*

minute hand　The *minute hand* is the long hand on a clock face. It shows how many minutes have passed in each hour.

- On some big clocks you can see the minutes passing as the *minute hand* jumps from one minute mark on the clock face to the next.

See *clock face*

missing　An item is *missing* if it is lost, or left out.

- Fill in the *missing* operation signs in these equations:

3 ☐ 7 = 10		3 + 7 = 10
14 ☐ 3 = 42		14 × 3 = 42
64 ☐ 8 = 8		64 ÷ 8 = 8
100 ☐ 100 = 0		100 − 100 = 0

mistake　A *mistake* is a wrong idea or a wrong answer.

- Gary understands the mathematics questions, but he often makes careless *mistakes* because he does not do the calculations slowly and carefully.

See *error*

mixed number　A *mixed number* is a number that contains a whole number and a fraction.

- $12\frac{1}{2}$ is a *mixed number*. It consists of the whole number 12 and the fraction $\frac{1}{2}$. It can also be written as the improper fraction $\frac{25}{2}$ or the decimal fraction 12,5.

See *decimal fraction; fraction; improper fraction; whole number*

mode　A *mode* is one type of average value used in statistics. An average is a measure of the most common events in a group of statistical data. The *mode* is the data event that occurs most often in the group.

- In a class test, 9 learners got the following marks:
  6, 5, 8, 12, 3, 5, 7, 7, 5
  The *mode* for this group of learners is therefore 5, because 5 occurs three times in the group of data. There is no other event that occurs more than three times in the group.

See *average; event; mean; median*

model　A *model* is a three-dimensional construction that shows how an object is built and how it works. The *model* is usually much smaller than the real object.

- Architects make *models* of new buildings as part of the planning process. The *models* allow them to show people how the new building will look, and how it will fit into the street where it will be constructed.

See *three-dimensional*

modulo arithmetic　*Modulo arithmetic* is a way of counting and calculating with a limited group of digits. The number of digits used is called the *modulo number n*, written as (mod *n*).

- *Arithmetic modulo 5* is arithmetic in which only the numbers 0, 1, 2, 3 and 4 are used. We can think of this as a 'clock' with only these numbers on the clock face. Then an addition like 3 + 4 (mod 5) means 'go 4 places forward from 3', which takes you to the position 2 on the clock face.

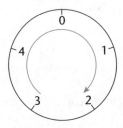

money   *Money* is the coins and paper notes (currency) that the government of a country issues as a way of paying for goods and services. The value of each coin and note is fixed by the government.

- The South African government issues *money* in the form of coins and notes. These are called 'legal tender'. No other coins or notes can be legally used as *money* in South Africa.

See *currency*

money order   A *money order* is a printed document that gives an instruction for an institution (such as a bank or the post office) to pay a certain amount of money to the person who owns the money order.

month, months of the year   A year is divided into groups of days, called *months*.

- In the calendar that South Africa and many other countries use, there are 12 *months* in one year. These *months* are: January, February, March, April, May, June, July, August, September, October, November, December.
  There are other ways of dividing a year into *months*. (See the examples on page 149 of this dictionary.)

See *calendar*

more   To have *more* of something means to add some of it to what you already have.

Hey, I want more too!

See *less*

monomial   A *monomial* is an algebraic expression with only one term. 'Mono-' means 'one'. Expressions with more than one term are called polynomials. 'Poly' means 'many'.

- The expression $32x^5$ is a *monomial* – it has only one term. $32x^5 + 2x$ is a polynomial because it has more than one term.

See *algebra; expression; polynomial; term*

more than   One quantity is *more than* another quantity if it has a greater numerical value.

- The mass of an elephant is *more than* the mass of a mouse.
- A car costs *more than* a bicycle.

morning   *Morning* is the part of the day from midnight (12.00 a.m.) until midday (12.00 p.m.).

- Many people go to work very early in the *morning*, when it is still dark outside.

See *afternoon; night*

most To have the *most* of something means to have the biggest amount or the highest quantity of it.

- Lindiwe has the *most* brothers and sisters of all the learners in the class. The other learners have 3 or 4 or 5 brothers and sisters, but Lindiwe has 12!

most expensive The *most expensive* item is the item that costs the most money.

- Simon's father bought the *most expensive* sound system in the shop.

mouse, mouse button (computer)
A computer *mouse* is a hand-held tool that is used to move the cursor (a little marker) on the computer screen. It is called a *mouse* because of its rounded shape and long cord that look like a *mouse's* body and tail.
A *mouse button* is a button on the top of the mouse that you push to give instructions to the computer.

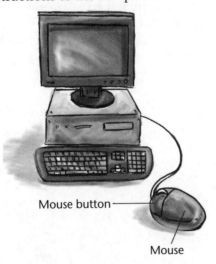

Mouse button

Mouse

multiple A number that is exactly divisible by another number (without any remainder) is a *multiple* of that number.

- 18 is a *multiple* of 9, because 18 is exactly divisible by 9:
  $18 \div 9 = 2$

See *lowest common multiple (LCM)*

multiplication, multiplication sign
Multiplication is a mathematical operation in which you add one number to itself many times. The *multiplication sign* (×) is the sign that we use for this operation.

- 6×5 means six multiplied by 5 or five 6s, which is the same as $6 + 6 + 6 + 6 + 6$.

multiplication table A *multiplication table* is a list of multiplication calculations for a particular number, giving the answers to the calculations. It is a useful way to remember the answers and use them in other calculations.
(See the *multiplication tables* on page 150 of this dictionary.)

multiplicative inverse The *multiplicative inverse* of any number is the number that, when multiplied with the first number, gives the answer 1. Zero does not have a *multiplicative inverse*.

- The *multiplicative inverse* of 5 is $\frac{1}{5}$, because $5 \times \frac{1}{5} = 1$. The *multiplicative inverse* of $\frac{1}{5}$ is 5, because $\frac{1}{5} \times 5 = 1$.

See *inverse operation*

multiply To *multiply* two numbers together means to add the first number to itself as many times as the second number indicates.

- To *multiply* 12 by 3 means to add 12 to itself 3 times: $12 \times 3 = 12 + 12 + 12 = 36$. We can use multiplication tables to find the answers to these 'repeated addition' calculations quickly, by remembering the answers given in the tables.

See *multiplication table*

N

narrow   A space or object is *narrow* if it has a small breadth (width).

- Some garages are too *narrow* for the big cars that people drive.
- Tumi hides his comics in the *narrow* space between his wardrobe and the wall.

See *breadth; broad; width*

natural numbers   The *natural numbers* are the numbers that we use for counting: 1, 2, 3, 4, ...
The set of all *natural numbers*
$N = \{1, 2, 3, 4, ...\}$ is an infinite set – there is no end to the *natural numbers*.
The number 0 is sometimes included in the set of *natural numbers*.

See *directed number; integer; rational number; real number; whole number*

nautical mile   A *nautical mile* is a measuring unit for distances at sea.
1 *nautical mile* is equal to 1 853,25 metres (or 1,85325 kilometres). This unit of distance was created by taking the distance between two lines of longitude along the equator that differ by 1°, and dividing this distance by 60.
A speed of 1 *nautical mile* per hour is known as 1 knot.

- The weather forecast for sailors gives the wind speed in knots. A wind speed of 30 knots means that the wind is blowing at 30 *nautical miles* per hour, which is equal to (30 × 1,85325) = 55,6 km/h (rounded to one decimal place).

See *metre*

near   Two places or objects are *near* each other if the distance or length between them is small.

- Suzette lives in Fordsburg, which is *near* to the Johannesburg city centre. She does not have to travel far to get to work.

See *far*

negative   A *negative* quantity is a quantity that is less than zero.

- Sutherland in the Karoo is one of the coldest places in South Africa. At night they often have *negative* temperatures as low as –8 °C or –9 °C.

See *positive*

negative integer   A *negative integer* is an integer (whole number) that is less than zero. The minus sign (–) is used to indicate that the integer is a *negative integer*. *Negative integers* are directed numbers that get bigger in the left direction on the number line.

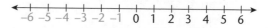

See *directed number; integer; positive number*

negative number   A *negative number*, quantity or integer, is one that is less than zero. It can be any kind of real number (integer, rational number, irrational number). *Negative numbers* are directed numbers: their value increases the further left they are on the number line.

- If you owe money to the bank, your bank statement will show the amount you owe as a *negative number* (a negative balance in your account). This means that you have an amount less than zero in your account, and you must first pay the amount back to the bank before you can add money to your account to have a positive balance.

Account summary	
Transaction summary	
Purchases/withdrawals	–R10 300,95
Payment + credit	R 8 000,00
Balance	– R 2 300,95
Amount owing	R 2 300,95

See *directed number; overdraft; positive number; real number*

neighbouring   1. People who live next door to each other are called neighbours. 2. *Neighbouring* keys on a computer or calculator keyboard are keys (buttons) that are next to each other.

- 8 and 9 are *neighbouring* keys on this calculator.

net   A *net* is a two-dimensional shape (a flat shape with length and breadth) that can be folded to make a three-dimensional object (with length, breadth and height). Every three-dimensional object has its own kind of *net*.

- These are *nets* for a cube, a cylinder and a pyramid.

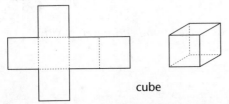

cube

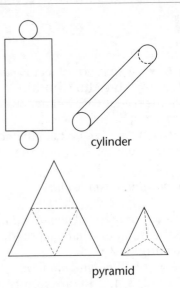

cylinder

pyramid

network   A *network* is a set of connected lines. The lines are called 'arcs'. The points at which the lines meet are called 'nodes'. The spaces between the lines are called 'regions'.

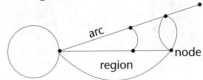

arc

node

region

next   The *next* item in a group is the nearest item to one that you are using or looking at – the item that comes immediately after it.

- The *next* natural number after 5 is 6.
- The *next* building after the school is a spaza shop.

night   *Night* is the time between sunset and sunrise, when it is dark outside.

- You should always drive with your lights on at *night*.

See *afternoon; morning*

nil   *Nil* means nought or zero.

- In the match between Kaizer Chiefs and Orlando Pirates the score was *nil-nil* – neither side scored a goal.

See *nought; zero*

nonagon   A *nonagon* is a polygon with nine sides. A regular *nonagon* has all its sides equal in length and all its interior angles equal to 140°.

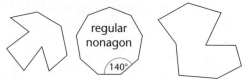

regular nonagon 140°

See *polygon*

non-collinear points   Collinear points are points that all lie on the same straight line. *Non-collinear* points are points that do not lie on the same straight line.

• The points E, F and G are *non-collinear points*.

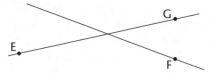

G
E
F

See *collinear points*

noon   *Noon* is another word for '12 o'clock midday'.

• The *Noon* Gun is a cannon on Signal Hill in Cape Town. It is fired every day except Sunday, at exactly 12 o'clock midday (12 *noon*). People in the city always check their watches when the gun fires.

See *midday*

north   *North* is one of the four cardinal (main) points of the compass. It is the directions opposite south on the compass.

not equal to   Two quantities are *not equal to* each other if they have different values.

• The amount of sugar in the small jar is *not equal to* the amount of sugar in the big jar.

nothing   *Nothing* is an ordinary (non-mathematical) term that means 'nought' or 'zero' – we use it to mean that there is 'no thing' or 'no value'.

nought   *Nought* means 'zero', the number with no value. The symbol for *nought* is 0. *Nought* is the number that lies between the negative numbers and the positive numbers on a number line.

• If you subtract a number from itself, you get *nought*:
$15 - 15 = 0$
$45\,000\,000 - 45\,000\,000 = 0$
$\frac{1}{4} - \frac{1}{4} = 0$

See *nil; zero*

null set   The *null set* is the empty set – that is, any set that has no elements. The symbol for the *null set* is { } or ∅.

• The set of all the animals that live on the moon is the *null set*. It has no elements, because there are no living creatures on the moon.

See *empty set*

number   A *number* is a concept for describing how many things there are. The first *numbers* were developed by people for counting real things in the world around them. Mathematicians use *numbers* to do calculations, without always linking the *numbers* to real objects.

• There are many different kinds of *numbers*, for example natural *numbers*, positive and negative *numbers*, rational *numbers*, real numbers and imaginary *numbers*.

• The Maya used a simple dot-and-dash method to represent *numbers*:

•	••	•••	••••	━━━
1	2	3	4	5

•	••	•••	••••	━━━
6	6	7	9	10

• Arabic numbers are written from right to left:

.٩٨٧٦٥٤٣٢١

number concept   A *number concept* is an abstract idea about what numbers are. All societies around the world have *number concepts*, and they express them using different number symbols and mathematical methods.

- The *number concept* for 'nothing' or 'zero' was difficult for many societies to understand. The first people to use zero were the Babylonians, but Indian mathematicians first started using the concept 'zero' in the way that we use it today.

number line   A *number line* is a line that shows a set of numbers arranged from left to right across the page. The numbers are given in order of size, from the numbers with the lowest values on the left to the numbers with the biggest values on the right.

- The directed numbers (negative and positive numbers) are shown on a *number line*:

- This *number line* shows quarters between 0 and 4:

$$0 \quad \tfrac{1}{4} \quad \tfrac{1}{2} \quad \tfrac{3}{4} \quad 1 \quad 1\tfrac{1}{4} \quad 1\tfrac{1}{2} \quad 1\tfrac{3}{4} \quad 2 \quad 2\tfrac{1}{4} \quad 2\tfrac{1}{2} \quad 2\tfrac{3}{4} \quad 3 \quad 3\tfrac{1}{4} \quad 3\tfrac{1}{2} \quad 3\tfrac{3}{4} \quad 4$$

See *directed number; rational number*

number pattern   A pattern is a regular (repeating) arrangement of things. A *number pattern* is a regular pattern that sometimes happens in a sequence of numbers. This pattern helps us to see that there is a rule for finding more numbers in the sequence.

- An example of a *number pattern* can be found in the sum of odd numbers:

  $1 = 1 = 1^2$
  $1 + 3 = 4 = 2^2$
  $1 + 3 + 5 = 9 = 3^2$
  $1 + 3 + 5 + 7 = 16 = 4^2$

  There seems to be a pattern here: we can conjecture (guess) that the sum of the first n odd numbers is n^2.

The pattern can be shown with a 'dot' diagram. The diagram suggests that the pattern continues for more odd numbers. We can use this pattern to develop a general algebraic proof to show that our conjecture 'the sum of the first n odd numbers is n^2' is true for all odd numbers.

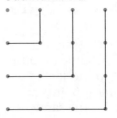

See *sequence*

number sentence   A *number sentence* is a sentence that uses numbers and other mathematical symbols to express a thought, instead of words.

- The *number sentence* $14 \div 2 = 7$ can also be expressed in words as 'fourteen divided by two equals seven'.

number symbol   A *number symbol* is a symbol (a visible sign) that expresses a number concept.

- We express the number concept 'two' by writing the *number symbol* 2. In the Roman number system this number concept is expressed by the symbol II or ii.

See *number concept; numeral*

number system   A *number system* is a collection of types of numbers and rules for using them to do calculations.

- In the base 10 *number system* we group numbers in powers of 10 (such as units, tens, hundreds, thousands) and we use place values to write the numbers.

See *base of a number; place value*

numeracy   *Numeracy* is the skill of being able to read and write numbers, and to do basic arithmetic calculations.

- We use *numeracy* skills to do lots of everyday things like go shopping, cook food, play games, and so on.

See *arithmetic*

numeral A *numeral* is a number symbol. Different societies use different *numerals* for the same number concept.

- In our number system we use the *numeral* 5 for the number concept 'five'. In the Roman number system the *numeral* V or v is used for this number concept.

numerate A *numerate* person is someone who has numeracy skills, and can read and write numbers and do everyday arithmetic calculations.

numerator The *numerator* of a fraction is the number above the division line. It tells you how many parts of the whole are in the fraction.

- In the fraction $\frac{3}{7}$, the *numerator* is 3. It tells you that the fraction expresses 3 parts of the whole. The bottom number, the denominator, tells you that the whole is divided into 7 parts.
- In the fractions:
  $$\frac{13}{19}, \frac{a}{b}, \frac{x^2}{2y}$$
  the numerators are 13, a and x^2.

See *denominator; fraction*

numerical information *Numerical information* is information about something that is given in the form of numbers and number sentences.

- The weather forecast uses *numerical information* such as temperatures, wind speeds and humidity levels to describe what the weather will be like.

Monthly accumulated rainfall recorded for the Free State province	
Month ending at 08:00 on Tuesday, 01 July 2008 (preliminary data)	
Free State	**Total rainfall (mm)**
Bethlehem Weather Office	10
Bloemfontein – City	37
Bloemfontein Weather Office	31
Bloemfontein Zoo	38
Winburg	22

numerous *Numerous* means 'consisting of many items'.

- There are *numerous* different hairstyles currently in fashion.

See *few*

object (transformations) The *object* of a transformation is the shape or set of points that is being transformed. The shape or set of points onto which the *object* is being transformed is called the 'image'.

- The shape ABCD is the *object* that has been transformed (enlarged). It has been enlarged from O with linear scale factor 2, to form shape A'B'C'D'. The shape A'B'C'D' is the image.

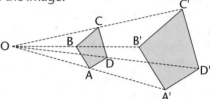

See *linear scale factor; transformation*

oblique An *oblique* line is a line that slants (slopes), and is not horizontal or vertical.

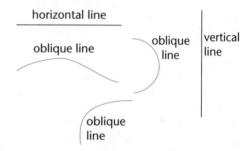

See *horizontal; vertical*

oblique cone or pyramid A cone or pyramid with its vertex directly above its base (that is, where a vertical line from the vertex meets the base at a right angle) is called a 'right cone' or a 'right pyramid'. If the vertex is not directly above the centre of the base, it is called an *oblique cone* or an *oblique pyramid*.

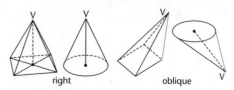

See *cone; pyramid*

oblong An *oblong* shape is a shape that has a length greater than its breadth.

• A rectangle has an *oblong* shape.

See *breadth; length; rectangle; square*

observe To *observe* something means to look closely at it, and study its properties scientifically.

• Ayla and Taine are doing a science project. They *observe* how the pigeons in the schoolyard behave, and write up their observations in detail. This gives them the information they need to describe how pigeons find food, build nests, and care for their babies.

obtuse angle An *obtuse angle* is an angle with a size that is greater than 90° and smaller than 180°.

See *angle; reflex angle*

obtuse triangle An *obtuse triangle* is a triangle that has one obtuse angle.

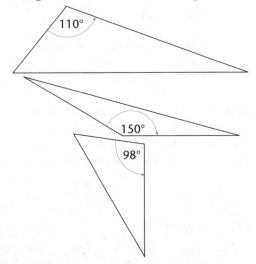

See *obtuse angle; triangle*

octa–, octagon, octahedron *Octa–* comes from the Greek word for 'eight'.
An *octagon* is a polygon (a flat shape) with eight sides.
An *octahedron* is a polyhedron (a solid shape) with eight plane faces.

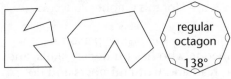

regular octagon

138°

See *polygon; polyhedron*

odd numbers An *odd number* is a number that cannot be divided by 2 exactly. The set of *odd numbers* is {1, 3, 5, 7, 9, 11, 13, …}. The negative integers {–1; –3; –5; –7; …} are also *odd numbers*. All *odd numbers* leave a remainder of 1 when they are divided by 2.

• Some examples of *odd numbers* are: 89, 467, 4 563, 36 821, 9 162 875

See *even numbers*

odds The *odds* of an event happening is a statistical measure of the chance that the event will happen. It is expressed as a ratio.

• A die has six faces numbered 1, 2, 3, 4, 5, 6. The *odds* against throwing a 3 when you roll the die is 5 to 1, because only one face has a 3, and there are six possible ways that the die can land. This is written as 1 : 6. The probability of throwing a 3 is 1 in 6.

See *event; probability*

odometer An *odometer* is an instrument for measuring how many kilometres a vehicle (such as a car or truck) has travelled. It is connected to the axle of the vehicle.

See *circumference*

ogive   An *ogive* is another name for a cumulative frequency diagram.

• This *ogive* shows the cumulative frequency of marks learners obtained in a test. It shows, for example, that 10 learners got 4 marks or less, and 26 learners got 7 marks or less.

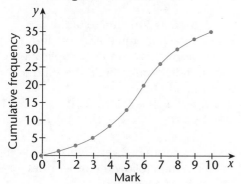

See *cumulative frequency*

once   *Once* means 'one time only'.

• Sizwe has been to the doctor only *once* this year. He is a very healthy person.

one-to-one correspondence   There is a *one-to-one correspondence* between two sets if every element in the first set maps onto only one element in the second set, by a one-to-one function.

• If there are two sets:
  E = {the set of natural numbers from 6 to 12}
  F = {the set of all numbers that are double the elements in E}
  then there is a *one-to-one correspondence* between set E and set F:
  E = {6, 7, 8, 9, 10, 11, 12}
  F = {12, 14, 16, 18, 20, 22, 24}
  We can show this as a one-to-one mapping:

E	F
6	→12
7	→14
8	→16
9	→18
10	→20
11	→22
12	→24

See *mapping*

operation   An *operation* is something that is done to mathematical quantities, to change them in some way.

The arithmetic *operations* are addition, subtraction, multiplication, division. The symbols for these *operations* are +, −, ×, ÷. Some other *operations* that we often use are finding the square root ($\sqrt{}$) or cube root ($\sqrt[3]{}$) of a number, and raising a number by a power (such as squaring or cubing the number).

Operations on sets are the intersection of sets (A ∩ B) and the union of sets (A ∪ B).

• In each of these calculations you must use a different *operation* to find the answer:
  $12 \times 12 = 144$
  $12 \div 12 = 1$
  $12 - 12 = 0$
  $12 + 12 = 24$

See *arithmetic; intersection of sets; power of a number; root of an equation; union of sets*

opposite   Two objects are *opposite* each other if they are face-to-face, with space between them.

• The supermarket is *opposite* the bookshop.

• In a rectangle, the two pairs of *opposite* sides are the same length.

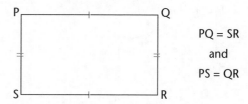

opposite angles   *Opposite angles* are angles directly across from each other in a shape. In some shapes, the *opposite angles* are equal.

• In the quadrilateral ABCD, the angle at A and the angle at C are *opposite angles*, and the angle at B and the angle at D are *opposite angles*.

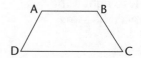

- In a parallelogram, both pairs of *opposite angles* are equal.

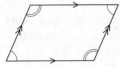

- In a kite, the *opposite angles* on either side of the line of symmetry are equal.

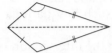

See *angle; kite; parallelogram*

opposite sides   *Opposite sides* are sides directly across from each other in a shape. In some shapes, the *opposite sides* are equal.

- In quadrilateral ABCD, side AD is opposite the side BC, and side DC is opposite the side AB. In this quadrilateral the *opposite sides* are not equal.

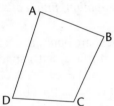

- In quadrilateral EFGH both pairs of *opposite sides* are equal.

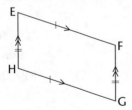

See *quadrilateral*

order of operations   The *order of operations* is a rule that tells you which mathematical operations to do first, second, third, and so on, in a calculation.

- Here are some rules for *order of operations* in arithmetic:
  - Work from left to right if the operations are all the same:
    15 + 17 + 12 = 44
    32 − 14 − 6 = 12
  - Work from left to right if there is addition and subtraction:
    26 + 8 − 14 = 20
    125 − 60 + 44 = 109
  - Work from left to right if there is multiplication and division:
    64 ÷ 16 × 7 = 28
    22 × 7 ÷ 11 = 14
  - If there is a mixture of addition, subtraction, multiplication and division, first do the multiplication and division, then do the subtraction and addition:
    6 + (5 × 2) = 6 + 10 = 16
    15 − (6 ÷ 2) + 7 = 15 − 3 + 7
    = 12 + 7 = 19
  - If there are brackets, work them out first, then follow the other rules for *order of operations*:
    25 − [(22 + 3) ÷ 5] = 25 − [25 ÷ 5]
    = 25 − 5 = 20

See *BODMAS*

ordered pair   An *ordered pair* is a pair of numbers in which the order of the numbers (which number comes first, and which number comes second) is important. *Ordered pairs* describe the position of a point on a Cartesian plane. The first number in the *ordered pair* gives the x-value of the number (the x-coordinate), and the second number gives the y-value of the number (the y-coordinate). *Ordered pairs* are written in round brackets, with a semi-colon between the two numbers: $(x; y)$.

- The point P on the graph is described by the *ordered pair* (2; 3). The point Q is described by the *ordered pair* (3; 2).

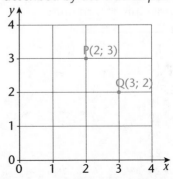

See *Cartesian plane; coordinates*

ordinal numbers *Ordinal numbers* describe the order or position of things in a group.

* Lerato sits in the sixth (6th) desk from the front of the class, in the second (2nd) row.

origin An *origin* is a starting point. It is the zero mark on a number line, or the point where coordinate axes cross on a graph. In two dimensions, it is the point with coordinates (0; 0) and in three dimensions it is the point with coordinates (0; 0; 0).

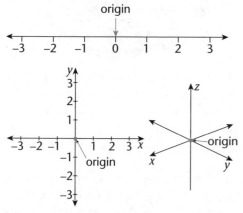

See *coordinates; number line*

orthocentre The *orthocentre* is the point where the three altitudes of a triangle meet.

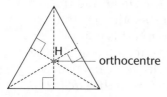

See *altitude of a triangle*

ounce An *ounce* is a unit for measuring mass in the imperial measuring system. There are 16 ounces in 1 pound. 1 *ounce* (abbreviation oz.) is equal to 28,35 grams in the metric measuring system.

See *gram; imperial units; metric system*

outcome An *outcome* is a word used in statistics for the result of an experiment.

* If three coins are tossed there are eight ways in which they could land with heads (H) or tails (T) uppermost. These are:

HHH HHT HTH THH HTT THT HTT TTT
These are the eight possible *outcomes* of the experiment.

See *statistics*

outlier An *outlier* is a word used in statistics to describe a point on a scatter diagram that lies far away from the other points on the diagram. It can also be used to describe a result of an experiment that is very different from all the other results of the experiment.

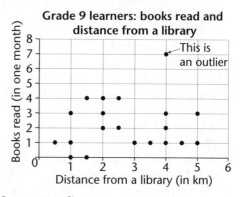

See *scatter diagram*

outside The *outside* of an object is its outer surface – the part that we can see without looking inside the object.
One object is *outside* another object if it is separate from the second object and in a different position.

* There is a label on the *outside* of the parcel.
* The point P lies *outside* the triangle ABC.

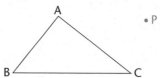

oval An *oval* is a curved shape like a flattened circle. There are two types of *oval*: one type has one line of symmetry, and looks like an egg; the other type has two lines of symmetry, and looks like an ellipse.

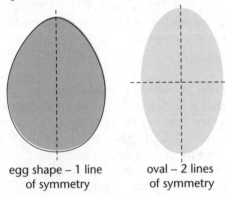

egg shape – 1 line   oval – 2 lines
of symmetry   of symmetry

See *circle; ellipse; line of symmetry*

overdraft An *overdraft* is an amount of money that the bank lets you borrow if you run out of money suddenly. The bank agrees that you can draw (take out) more money than you have in your account, as long as you pay interest on this *overdraft*.

• Linda has an *overdraft* agreement with the bank. If she needs more money than she has in her account, she can borrow up to R5 000 extra from the bank. But she has to pay a high interest rate on this *overdraft* to the bank, so she tries to plan her spending so that she never needs to use it.

See *bank account*

P

pair A *pair* is a set of two things that are usually found together or used together.

• These things usually come in *pairs*:

• An ordered *pair* of coordinates on a graph consists of two numbers $(x; y)$ that give the x- and y-values of a particular point.

See *coordinates; ordered pair*

pair of compasses A *pair of compasses* is often incorrectly called a compass. It is an instrument used in geometry to draw circles. It has two legs. One leg has a sharp point at the tip; the other leg holds a pen or pencil. The sharp point marks the centre of the circle, and the pencil on the other leg rotates around this point to draw the circumference of the circle. You can change the size of the circle by making the gap between the two legs bigger or smaller.

See *arc of a circle; circumference; geometry; mathematical instruments*

palindrome, palindromic A *palindrome* is a word or sentence that reads the same backwards and forwards. A *palindromic number* is a number that reads the same backwards and forwards.

• Words that are *palindromes*:
mom, dad, toot, pip, pop, pup, peep, refer.

- Sentences that are *palindromes*:
  Madam, I'm Adam.
  Able was I ere I saw Elba.
- Examples of *palindromic numbers*:

parabola   A *parabola* is the curve that is described by the quadratic function $y = ax^2 + bx + c$. If this function is plotted as a graph on a Cartesian plane, the shape of the graph is a *parabola*.

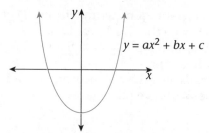

$$y = ax^2 + bx + c$$

- If an object such as a ball is thrown through the air, the path it follows has approximately the shape of a *parabola*.

See *Cartesian plane; graph; quadratic function*

parallel   *Parallel* lines are two or more straight lines that never meet, no matter how far they extend. The vertical distance between any two *parallel* lines is always the same. To indicate that lines are *parallel*, small arrows are drawn on them. The symbol for *parallel* is ||.

- The lines on a sheet of writing paper are *parallel*.
- Railway tracks are *parallel*.

See *line*

parallelogram   A *parallelogram* is a quadrilateral with both pairs of opposite sides parallel. The opposite sides of a *parallelogram* are equal in length, and the opposite angles are equal. The diagonals cut each other in half.

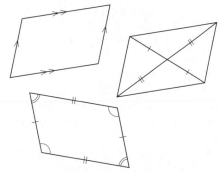

See *parallel; quadrilateral*

part   A *part* of an object is a section of it, not the whole thing.

- All the *parts* will together make a bicycle.

See *fraction*

partition   See *break up*

Pascal's triangle   *Pascal's triangle* is a number pattern. It is named after a French mathematician, Blaise Pascal (1623–1662), who described this pattern in numbers. (He also invented the first mechanical computer.) The pattern in *Pascal's triangle* starts with a 1 at the vertex. It has a 1 at each end of every row below the vertex. Each other number in a row is calculated as the sum of the two numbers immediately above it. This triangular pattern is important in algebra and probability calculations.

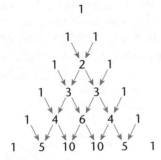

See *triangle; vertex*

path In mathematics, a *path* is another name for a route around a network or in space.
- The putt putt ball follows a certain *path* before sinking into the hole:

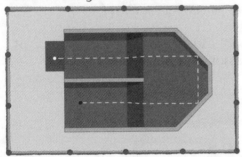

See *network*

pattern A *pattern* is a group of numbers, shapes or other symbols that is arranged according to certain rules. In a *pattern*, there is some property that repeats itself – it can be the order of shapes, or the calculation rules, or some other property of the elements of the *pattern*.
- The multiplication tables can be set out in the form of *patterns* like this triangular *pattern*:

```
1
2   4
3   6   9
4   8   12 16
5   10  15 20 25
6   12  18 24 30 36
7   14  21 28 35 42 49
8   16  24 32 40 48 56 64
9   18  27 36 45 54 63 72 81
10  20  30 40 50 60 70 80 90  100
11  22  33 44 55 66 77 88 99  110 121
12  24  36 48 60 72 84 96 108 120 132 144
```

- *Patterns* occur in many natural objects:

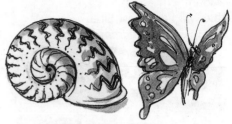

- *Patterns* are an important part of many objects designed by people:

penta–, pentagon, pentahedron *Penta–* comes from the Greek word for 'five'.
A *pentagon* is a polygon (a flat shape) with five sides.
A *pentahedron* is a polyhedron (a solid shape) with five plane faces.

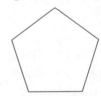

See *polygon; polyhedron*

pentagram A *pentagram* is a five-pointed star. It is the shape formed by the diagonals of a regular pentagon.
- A starfish has the approximate shape of a *pentagram*.

See *pentagon*

per cent, percentage   *Per cent* means 'per 100'. A *percentage* is a way of expressing a fraction as so many parts out of 100 parts. The symbol for *per cent* is %.

- Any fraction can be converted to a *percentage* by finding an equivalent fraction with the denominator 100.
  $\frac{1}{4} = \frac{25}{100}$. This can be written as 25%.
  $\frac{3}{8} = (\frac{3}{8} \times 100)\% = 37{,}5\%$
- Any *percentage* can be converted to a fraction by dividing by 100.
  $47\% = \frac{47}{100}$
  $30\% = \frac{30}{100} = \frac{3}{10}$

See *denominator; fraction*

percentage change   A *percentage change* is the amount by which a given number decreases or increases, expressed as a percentage of the number.

- In December some beach umbrellas were on sale for R50 each. In May, the shopkeeper reduced the price to R20 each. The reduction in price was R30. This is a *percentage change* of $\frac{30}{50} \times \frac{100}{1} = 60\%$.

See *per cent; percentage; price*

percentile   A *percentile* is a special data item within a group of data. Sometimes a large group of data is arranged in order by size and then divided into 100 equal groups, with the groups rising from the smallest data in the 1st group to the biggest data in the 100th group. When this happens, the data at the boundaries of the groups are called the *percentiles*.

- Imagine that all the people who live in Johannesburg stand in a line, with the youngest person first and the oldest person last. If 15% of the people in the line are 9 years old or younger, then 9 years is the 15th *percentile*. If 33% of the people are 25 years or younger, then 25 is the 33rd *percentile*.

See *data; per cent; percentage*

perfect number   A *perfect number* is a whole number that is equal to the sum of all its factors (not including itself).

- The two smallest *perfect numbers* are 6 and 28:
  Factors of 6: 1, 2, 3, 6
  6 = 1 + 2 + 3
  Factors of 28: 1, 2, 4, 7, 14, 28
  28 = 1 + 2 + 4 + 7 + 14

See *factor; whole number*

perfect square   A *perfect square* is any number that is equal to the square of a whole number. All *perfect squares* can be represented (shown) as a square array of dots.

- The first five square numbers are:
  $1 = 1^2; 4 = 2^2; 9 = 3^2;$
  $16 = 4^2; 25 = 5^2$

$16 = 4 \times 4$

See *array; square; whole number*

perimeter   The *perimeter* of a two-dimensional shape is the total length of its boundary (edge). The abbreviation for *perimeter* is P.

- The *perimeter* of a piece of land is the total length that you would walk if you walked all around the edge of the land. In this example,
  P = 25 + 25 + 35 + 40 + 30 = 155 m.

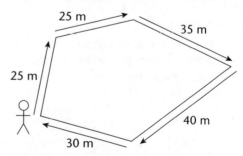

See *length; two-dimensional*

per month   *Per month* means 'happening every month'. An event that happens three times *per month* is one that happens three times every month.

- Desmond goes to visit his grandfather four times *per month*.

See *month*

permutation   A *permutation* is a rearrangement of the objects in a group.
- If there are three children, Alice (A), Bhuti (B) and Carel (C), who want to sit on three chairs in a row, then they can choose to sit in six different arrangements (orders) on the chairs:
ABC BCA CAB BAC CBA ACB.
These are the six *permutations* of seating order for these three children.

Alice   Bhuti   Carel

perpendicular   *Perpendicular* means 'at right angles'. Two lines are *perpendicular* if they meet or cut each other at an angle of 90°. The symbol ⊥ is used to show that two lines are *perpendicular* to each other.

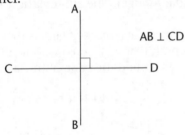

AB ⊥ CD

- A line can be *perpendicular* to a plane: the edge where two walls of a room meet is a line that meets the plane of the floor at 90°.

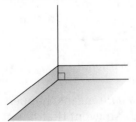

- Two planes can be *perpendicular*: two walls of a room with a common edge, or two sides of a box with a common edge, are *perpendicular* planes.

See *edge; plane; right angle*

perpendicular bisector   A *perpendicular bisector* is a line that is drawn at right angles (perpendicular) to a line segment, which cuts the line segment exactly in half (bisects it).

See *bisect; line segment*

perspective   *Perspective* is the relative distance, size and proportion of objects as they are seen from a particular point.
- In this drawing, the buildings are drawn in *perspective* so that the buildings far away look smaller than the ones that are nearer.

perspective drawing   A *perspective drawing* gives a three-dimensional effect to a two-dimensional drawing: it lets the viewer think that she is looking 'through' the drawing to a point somewhere behind the flat paper.

pi   When the length of the circumference of any circle is divided by the length of its diameter, the result is always the same number, called *pi*. The symbol for this number is the Greek letter π, which is pronounced *pi*.
$$\frac{C}{d} = \pi \text{ or } C = \pi d$$
This is true for all circles.
The value of *pi* is slightly more than 3. It is an irrational number, and its exact value has never been calculated. Mathematicians have found its value up to billions of decimal places. In everyday calculations we usually say that the value of *pi* is 3,142 or $\frac{22}{7}$.

- *Pi* is used to calculate the area and the circumference of a circle:
  Area = πr^2
  Circumference = $2\pi r$
  where *r* is the radius of the circle.

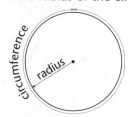

See *circumference; diameter; irrational number*

pictogram   A *pictogram* is a way of representing statistical data using pictures, so that the data can be easily understood. The pictures represent the frequency of the different types of data events.

- This *pictogram* shows the results of a survey of the transport the learners use to get to school. Each large symbol represents 2 vehicles. A small symbol represents 1 vehicle. The *pictogram* shows that in this class, 10 learners travel by car, 13 by bus and 9 by bicycle.

car	🚗🚗🚗🚗🚗				10
bus	🚌🚌🚌🚌🚌🚌🚌			🚌	13
bicycle	🚲🚲🚲🚲	🚲			9

pie chart   A *pie chart* is a way of showing statistical data in the form of a diagram (picture) so that the data are easy to understand. The total quantity of data is represented by a complete circle (or pie). The circle is divided up into sectors (pieces of the pie) in proportion to the frequencies of the data. The size of the angle at the centre of the pie for each sector totals 360°, and is in the same ratio as the data.

- This *pie chart* shows the proportion of learners who travel by car, bus or bicycle. The data here is the same as the data shown in the pictogram entry before.

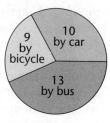

See *proportion*

PIN (personal identification number)
Your *PIN* code allows you access to the money in your bank account when you use your debit or credit card. Never tell anyone else what your *PIN* code is.

See *autobank*

pint   A *pint* is a unit for measuring volume or capacity in the imperial measuring system. There are 8 pints in 1 gallon. 1 litre is equal to approximately 1,76 pints.

See *gallon; imperial units; litre*

place value   A *place value* number system is a system in which a number changes its value, depending on the position (place) of the digits in the number. Each place in the system is linked to the powers of the base used in that system.

- Our number system is a base 10 system. Each place in this system represents a power of 10:
  units (10^0)
  tens (10^1)
  hundreds (10^2)
  thousands (10^3)
  and so on.
- The digit 5 has different values in the following numbers, because it is in different places:
  In 105: its value is 5
  In 157: its value is 50
  In 583: its value is 500
  In 12,50: its value is 0,5 or $\frac{5}{10}$

See *base of a number; decimal*

plane   A *plane* is a flat surface, like a sheet of glass or a table top. It can be vertical, horizontal or oblique. In mathematics a *plane* is a two-dimensional shape with length and breadth, but no height, that is imagined as stretching forever in all directions, with no edges.

• The Cartesian *plane* is a two-dimensional surface on which we plot points and join them to show the graphs of equations.

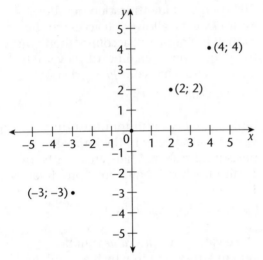

See *Cartesian plane; horizontal; oblique; vertical*

plane figure   A *plane figure* is a shape that has two dimensions, length and breadth, but no height.

• Triangles, rectangles and all other polygons are *plane figures*.

See *polygon; rectangle; triangle*

plan view   A *plan view* is a diagram of a place or an object that shows how it looks from directly above it – as if you were looking at it from a plane flying overhead.

• This is a *plan view* of part of the Cape Town harbour.

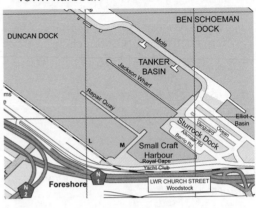

Platonic solids   The *Platonic solids* are the five regular polyhedra: the cube, the regular tetrahedron, the regular octahedron, the regular dodecahedron (12 faces) and the regular icosahedron (20 faces). All the faces of each *Platonic solid* are regular polygons, and the same number of edges meet at each vertex of the solid. They are named after the Greek philosopher Plato, who argued that there were certain forms (shapes) that expressed ideals of perfection.

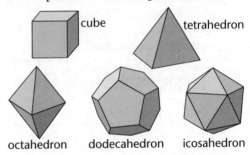

See *polyhedron; regular polyhedron*

plus   The *plus* symbol (+) is used in two different ways in mathematics:

• When written between two numbers, it is the sign for addition.

• When written just before a number, it shows that the number is positive (greater than zero), in contrast to a negative number (a number less than zero).

• 'Three *plus* twelve' can be written as 3 + 12.

• 'Positive 26' can be written as +26.

p.m. (*post meridiem*)   The letters *p.m.* stand for the Latin words *post meridiem*, which mean 'after noon'. We use these letters to describe the time between 12 o'clock midday and 12 o'clock midnight on an analogue clock.

- The day shift at the factory ends at 6 *p.m.*

See *a.m.; analogue clock*

point   A *point* is a position in space. It has no length, breadth or height. The exact position of the *point* can be described by giving its coordinates. We usually represent a *point* on a diagram by means of a dot.

- The *point* B on the Cartesian plane is at the position (3, 7).

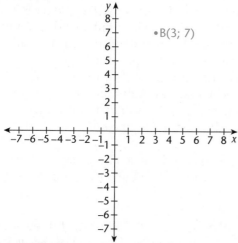

See *coordinates*

points of the compass   The *points of the compass* are the different directions shown on the compass. There are four main compass points: north, south, east and west. There are usually 16 points marked on the compass face.

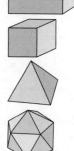

See *compass (magnetic)*

polygon   A *polygon* is a closed plane figure whose boundary is formed by three or more straight lines. It has two dimensions, length and breadth, but no height. Many *polygons* have special names, which refer to the number of lines forming their boundaries. A regular *polygon* is a polygon with all its sides the same length, and all its interior angles the same size.

- Rectangles and pentagons are examples of *polygons*.

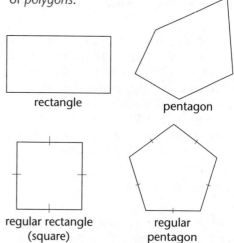

rectangle   pentagon

regular rectangle   regular
(square)   pentagon

See *plane figure; regular polygon*

polyhedron (plural: polyhedra)   A *polyhedron* is a three-dimensional shape (length, breadth and height) whose faces are all polygons. Many *polyhedra* have special names that correspond to the number or type of faces they have.

- A cuboid has 6 rectangular faces.

- A cube has 6 square faces.

- A regular tetrahedron has 4 equilateral triangles as its faces.

- A regular icosahedron has 20 equilateral triangles as its faces.

See *face; polygon*

polynomial   A *polynomial* is a type of algebraic expression in which each term consists of a constant multiplied by a power of a variable. 'Poly-' means 'many', and in a *polynomial* there are always two or more such terms.
- Examples of *polynomials*:
  - $2x^3 + 5x^2 - 8x + 1$
  - $y^2 - 7y + 6$
  - $4z + 3x$

See *algebra; expression; monomial; power of a number; term; variable*

population   In statistics, a *population* is the group of people or objects or other items that is being studied. Data are collected about this *population*, and analysed using statistical methods.
- In a study of animal breeding patterns in the Kruger National Park, the *population* consisted of elephants, giraffe and leopard.

See *data*

positive   A *positive* quantity is a quantity that is more than zero.
- Your age will always be a *positive* number.

See *negative*

positive number   A *positive number* is any number greater than zero. On a number line, *positive numbers* are shown to the right of the zero mark. A plus sign can be used to show that a number is a *positive number*, but it is often left out.
- Examples of *positive numbers* are:
  +6
  +7,5
  +9 861
  +0,333333

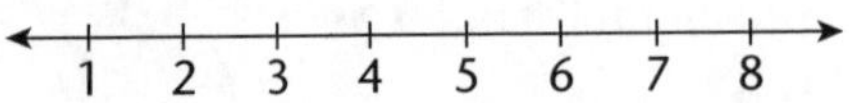

See *negative number; number line; plus*

postal code   Every city, suburb, town and village in South Africa has its own *postal code* number. The post office uses these numbers to sort letters into the correct areas.

- When you post a letter to someone you must always write the person's full address and *postal code* number on the envelope.

pound   A *pound* is a unit for measuring mass in the imperial measuring system. 1 *pound* is equal to 16 ounces. A *pound* is approximately equal to 454 grams.

See *imperial units*

power of a number   If a number x is multiplied by itself, the *power of the number* shows how many times x is multiplied in this way. The power is written as a small number (index) above the number being multiplied. This is read as 'x to the power of ...'
For the powers of 2 and 3 there are special names: A number multiplied *to the power of* 2 is squared. A number multiplied *to the power of* 3 is cubed.
- $5 \times 5 = 5^2$
  This is 5 multiplied by itself twice, which is read as '5 to the power of 2' or '5 squared'.
- $12 \times 12 \times 12 = 12^3$
  This is 12 multiplied by itself three times, which is read as '12 to the power of 3' or '12 cubed'.
- $7 \times 7 \times 7 \times 7 = 7^4$
  This is 7 multiplied by itself four times, which is read as '7 to the power of 4'.

See *index*

practise   To *practise* doing something means to keep doing it over and over to improve your skill.
- The only way to learn how to ride a bicycle is to *practise* every day, until you learn how to keep your balance.
- If you *practise* doing arithmetic calculations, you will soon improve your accuracy and speed, and your answers will be more correct.

precise To be *precise* means to give an exact and accurate answer to a question.
- If you phone the Talking Clock by dialling 1026, you will hear a voice giving the *precise* time every ten seconds of the day.

predict To *predict* something means to say what you think will happen in the future, using all the information you have at present.
- Farmers can often *predict* what the weather will be in the next few days by using information like the colour of the mountains, the way the insects and birds are behaving, or the way the wind is blowing.

previous Something is *previous* if it happens before something else in time, or comes before it in a list.
- On Friday Siphokazi did not go to swimming practice. The *previous* day, on Thursday, she had trained in the pool for three hours, so she stayed at home and rested.

price The *price* of something is the amount of money you must pay to buy it.
- The *price* of a new cellphone is very high. It can cost as much as R3 000.

See *cost price; selling price*

prime factors The factors of a number are the numbers that can divide exactly into that number, without leaving any remainder. The *prime factors* are the factors that are prime numbers.
Every number can be written as a product (multiplication) of its *prime factors*.
- The factors of 36 are 1, 2, 3, 4, 6, 9, 12, 18 and 36. Two of these numbers are prime numbers, namely 2 and 3. These are called *prime factors* of 36.
- 36 can be written as a product of its *prime factors*, 2 and 3:
  $$36 = 2 \times 18$$
  $$= 2 \times 2 \times 9$$
  $$= 2 \times 2 \times 3 \times 3$$

- $46 = 2 \times 23$ (where 2 and 23 are both prime numbers)
  $$96 = 2 \times 48$$
  $$= 2 \times 2 \times 24$$
  $$= 2 \times 2 \times 2 \times 12$$
  $$= 2 \times 2 \times 2 \times 2 \times 6$$
  $$= 2 \times 2 \times 2 \times 2 \times 2 \times 3$$

See *factor; prime number*

prime number A *prime number* is a number that has only two factors: itself and 1. No other number will divide into it exactly.
1 is not a *prime number*.
The only even *prime number* is 2.
There are infinitely many *prime numbers*.
Any number can be written as a product of *prime numbers* (which are called the prime factors of the number).
- The first ten *prime numbers* are 2, 3, 5, 7, 11, 13, 17, 19, 23, 29

See *prime factors*

principal A *principal* is an amount of money (also called the 'capital') that you borrow from a bank or business, or that you invest in a business. When you repay money that you have borrowed, you must repay not only this *principal* amount but also the interest owing on the loan.
- Lebogang borrowed money from the bank and now she must pay back a total amount of R5 456. The *principal* that she borrowed was R5 000. She also owes R456 in interest charges on the *principal*.

See *interest; invest*

principle A *principle* is a scientific or mathematical law that explains a natural process.
- The *principle* of gravity is the reason why all things on Earth are attracted to the centre of the Earth, instead of floating away into space.

prism   A *prism* is a solid shape whose cross-sections parallel to one end of the *prism* are all the same shape. The volume (V) of any *prism* is equal to the area of its cross-section *A* multiplied by its height *h*: V = Ah.

- The cross-sections of these *prisms* are shaded in each diagram:

See *cross-section; volume*

probability   The *probability* of a statistical outcome (result) is a number value that says how likely (probable) it is that the outcome will happen. The *probability* of getting a certain outcome is calculated by taking the number of possible events that can give that outcome, and dividing it by the total number of outcomes.

- In a standard pack of playing cards there are 52 cards, and four of these cards are kings. Therefore the *probability* that if you take one card from the pack, it will be a king, is $\frac{4}{52}$.
- A coin has two faces, heads and tails. When a coin is tossed there are two possible outcomes: it can land on either heads or tails. So if you toss a coin, the *probability* that you will get heads is $\frac{1}{2}$, and the *probability* that you will get tails is also $\frac{1}{2}$.

See *event; outcome*

proceed   To *proceed* means 'to carry on' or 'to do the next step in the task'.

- When you have done the arithmetic section of the test, you can *proceed* to do the geometry diagrams.

process   A *process* is a method of carrying out a task, or an organised way of doing something.

- The *process* for getting an ID document is quite long. You first have to get a form and fill it in. Then you have to go to the Department of Home Affairs and hand in the form. Then you have to wait for the ID document to be ready, and then go back to the Department of Home Affairs to collect your ID document. For each part of the *process* you have to wait in a long queue.

product   In mathematics, a *product* is the result of a multiplication calculation.

- The *product* of 25 and 34 is 850.
  25 × 34 = 850

See *multiplication*

profit   *Profit* is the amount of money that you make if you sell an item for more money than you paid for it. *Profit* is calculated as:
selling price – cost price.

- Sam bought a DVD player for R850 in East London. He took it back home to Cradock and sold it for R925. He made a *profit* of R75.

See *cost price; selling price*

program   A *program* is a set of instructions given to a computer to get it to carry out a group of tasks.

- There are computer *programs* that can do complicated mathematical calculations very quickly.

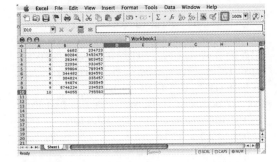

proof, prove   A *proof* is a step-by-step argument that shows how a certain mathematical result will always be true. To *prove* a result means to construct a *proof* to show that it is true.

- Here is one *proof* that two triangles are congruent when two angles and a corresponding side are used.

Prove that △EFO ≡ △GHO.

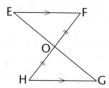

In △EFO and △GHO:
1) EÔF = GĤO   (alternate ∠s, EF ∥ HG)
2) FÔE = HÔG   (vertically opp ∠s are equal)
3) FO = HO   (given)
∴ △EFO ≡ △GHO   (two angles, corresp. side are equal)

proper fraction   A *proper fraction* is a fraction in which the numerator (the number at the top) is smaller than the denominator (the number at the bottom).

• $\frac{3}{4}$, $\frac{100}{144}$ and $\frac{7}{301}$ are all examples of *proper fractions*.

See *fraction*

properties   *Properties* are facts that are always true about a set of numbers, geometrical shapes, or transformations.

• A *property* of even numbers is that 2 is a factor of any even number.
• A *property* of a rhombus is that its diagonals intersect at right angles.
• Some of the *properties* of a cube are:
  ‣ It has six faces.
  ‣ All its faces are squares of equal size.
  ‣ All its corners (vertices) are right angles.

proportion, proportional to   Two sequences of numbers are *proportional to* each other if the one sequence of numbers is a constant times bigger or smaller than the other set.
Two shapes are in *proportion* to each other if the parts of the one shape are all a constant times bigger or smaller than the parts of the other shape.

• The sets A = {2, 4, 6, 8} and B = {6, 12, 18, 24} are *proportional to* each other, because the numbers in B are all 3 times the numbers in set A.
• These two triangles are in *proportion*, because the lengths of the sides of triangle DEF are all 2 times the lengths of the sides of triangle ABC. (Triangles that are in *proportion* are called 'similar triangles'.)

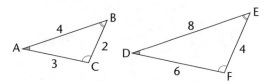

See *constant*

protractor   A protractor is an instrument for measuring the size of angles and drawing angles of a given size.

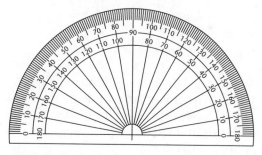

See *angle*

purchase   To *purchase* something means to buy it.
• Usually if you want to *purchase* a house you need to borrow a large sum of money from the bank.

See *buy*

puzzle   A *puzzle* is a game or toy that tests your skill at solving problems.
• In a jigsaw *puzzle*, you have to fit the pieces together correctly.
• In a Rubik's Cube *puzzle*, you have to move the squares around the cube to make each face have the same colour squares.

pyramid   A *pyramid* is a polyhedron formed by joining the edges of a polygon to a point to form sloping triangular faces. The polygon forms the base of the *pyramid*.

- The *pyramids* of Egypt have square bases.

These *pyramids* have a pentagonal and a triangular base.

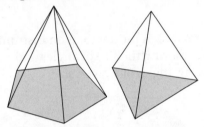

See *polygon; polyhedron*

Pythagoras' theorem   Pythagoras was a Greek mathematician who lived in about 500 BCE. He proved an important fact about right-angled triangles: the area of the square on the side opposite the right angle of the triangle (the hypotenuse), is equal to the sum of the areas of the squares on the two sides that form the right angle.
Area C = area A + area B.

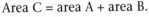

He proved that this is true for every right-angled triangle. His proof is known as *Pythagoras' theorem*.

The theorem can be written in algebraic form as $c^2 = a^2 + b^2$, where a, b and c are the lengths of the sides of the triangle, and c is the hypotenuse.

- *Pythagoras' theorem* can be used to find the length of a side in a right-angled triangle if the lengths of the other two sides are known.

In triangle PQR:

the theorem says that $PQ^2 = QR^2 + PR^2$.
So $QR^2 = PQ^2 - PR^2$
$$= 100 - 36$$
$$= 64$$
$$= 8^2$$
Therefore QR = 8.

See *hypotenuse; right-angled triangle; theorem*

Pythagorean triples   A triple is a group of three things. A *Pythagorean triple* is a group of three numbers a, b and c that satisfies (fits) Pythagoras' theorem: $c^2 = a^2 + b^2$.

- Some well-known *Pythagorean triples* are:
3, 4, 5: $5^2 = 3^2 + 4^2$
5, 12, 13: $13^2 = 5^2 + 12^2$
8, 15, 17: $17^2 = 8^2 + 15^2$
7, 24, 25: $25^2 = 24^2 + 7^2$

There are infinitely many *Pythagorean triples*.

Q

quadrangle, quadrangular   A *quadrangle* is an open space between buildings, and is in the shape of a rectangle. Quadrilaterals are sometimes called *quadrangles*. 'Quad' is sometimes used as an abbreviation for *quadrangle*.

- The courtyard inside a school building is often a *quadrangle*.

See *quadrilateral*

quadrant   A *quadrant* is one of the four equal sectors of a circle that are obtained when two diameters cut the circle at right angles.

- The x-axis and the y-axis of a Cartesian plane divide the plane into four *quadrants*. They are numbered 1st, 2nd, 3rd and 4th *quadrants*, as shown in the diagram.
  - In the 1st *quadrant* all values of x and y are positive.
  - In the 2nd *quadrant* all values of x are negative, all values of y are positive.
  - In the 3rd *quadrant* all values of x are negative, all values of y are negative.
  - In the 4th *quadrant* all values of x are positive, all values of y are negative.

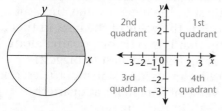

See *Cartesian plane; diameter; right angle; sector of a circle*

quadratic equation   A *quadratic equation* is an equation that can be written in the form $ax^2 + bx + c = 0$, where a, b and c are constant values, $a \neq 0$ and x is a variable. The word 'quadratic' refers to the fact that the variable x is squared (raised to the power 2). In a *quadratic equation* the highest power of the variable is 2. A *quadratic equation* can have two solutions – that is, there are two values of x that will make the equation true, or it can have only one solution, or none at all.

- These are examples of *quadratic equations*:
  $4x^2 = 9$ (or, in the form $ax^2 + bx + c = 0$:
  $4x^2 + 0x + -9 = 0$
  Solutions:
  $4x^2 = 9$
  $x^2 = \dfrac{9}{4}$
  $x = \dfrac{3}{2}$ or $x = -\dfrac{3}{2}$
  These are the two solutions of the equation.

- $2x^2 - 5x + 2 = 0$
  Solutions:
  $2x^2 - 5x + 2 = 0$
  $(2x - 1)(x - 2) = 0$
  So $(2x - 1) = 0$ or $(x - 2) = 0$
  $2x - 1 = 0$ which means $2x = 1$,
  therefore $x = \dfrac{1}{2}$.
  $x - 2 = 0$ which means $x = 2$.
  These are the two solutions of the equation.

See *constant; equation; parabola; power of a number; variable*

quadratic function   A *quadratic function* is a polynomial function in which the highest power of the variable is 2. The most general form of the *quadratic function* is $y = ax^2 + bx + c$ where a, b and c are constant values, $a \neq 0$ and x is a variable.

- The graphs of parabolas are described by the *quadratic function*. The parabola on the next page is the graph of the *quadratic function* $y = x^2 - 4x + 3$.

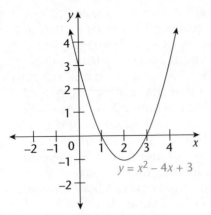

$y = x^2 - 4x + 3$

See *function; parabola; polynomial; power of a number; variable*

quadrilateral   A *quadrilateral* is a polygon with four sides, and four angles that add up to 360°. The prefix 'quad-' always means 'four'. There are many kinds of quadrilaterals with special features, which have their own names.
- Some examples of *quadrilaterals*:

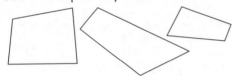

- Some examples of *quadrilaterals* with special features:

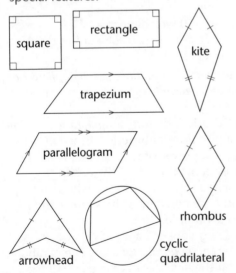

See *polygon*

quantity   A *quantity* is an amount of something that can be counted, measured to find its size, or weighed to find its mass.
- 12 marbles, 325 metres of ribbon, 500 grams of butter and 7 tonnes of bricks are all *quantities*.

quarter   A *quarter* is one of four equal parts of a whole shape or quantity. One *quarter* is written as $\frac{1}{4}$.

- A litre of milk can be divided into *quarters* of 250 ml each.
- The number 100 can be divided into *quarters*: 100 ÷ 4 = 25 (25 + 25 + 25 + 25)

See *fraction*

quarter past, quarter to   1 hour is 60 minutes long. A quarter of an hour is therefore 60 ÷ 4 = 15 minutes. A *quarter past* the hour means 15 minutes after the last full hour. A *quarter to* means 15 minutes before the next full hour. A *quarter to* can also be written as 45 minutes after the last full hour.
- The next train leaves at a *quarter past* 11 in the morning; that is, 11.15 a.m.
- Busi's appointment with the dentist is at a *quarter to* 4 this afternoon; that is 3.45 p.m.

See *quarter*

quartile   If the items in a set of statistical data are arranged in order from the smallest to the biggest value, then the *quartile* is the value of the item in the group that is exactly one quarter along the order from smallest to biggest. *Quartiles* are used in statistics to describe the value of data items at quarterly intervals in the data set.

See *data*

questionnaire A *questionnaire* is a list of questions that is used to collect information on a particular topic. This information is then analysed in more detail using statistical methods.

- Sometimes a *questionnaire* contains boxes that must be ticked to show which is the correct information.

quinary 'Quin' means 'five'. A *quinary* number system is a number system that uses base 5. A *quinary* arrangement of things is an arrangement that groups the things in fives.

See *base of a number; number system*

quiz A *quiz* is a competition that tests people's knowledge about a particular subject, in an entertaining way. It is usually held in front of an audience.

- At the end of the school year the teachers organise a *quiz* for the learners. The questions are all about sports and entertainment. The class that answers the most questions correctly wins a prize.

quotient A *quotient* is the whole number part of the answer to a division calculation.

- In the division calculation 589 ÷ 17, the answer is 34,647059. The *quotient* part of this answer is 34.
- In the division calculation 2 000 ÷ 40, the answer is 50. The *quotient* is 50.

See *whole number*

R

radius A *radius* of a circle is any straight line drawn from the centre of the circle to a point on its circumference. The plural of *radius* is 'radii'.

- The *radius* of a bicycle wheel is found by measuring the length of any of its radii.

circumference

See *circumference*

raising to a power *Raising to a power* means calculating a number to the given power, by multiplying the number by itself as many times as the power indicates.

- To *raise 2 to the power 6* means to calculate 2^6. This is done by multiplying 2 by itself 6 times:
  $2^6 = 2 \times 2 \times 2 \times 2 \times 2 \times 2 = 64$

See *power of a number*

rand The *rand* is a unit of money in South Africa. One rand is equal to 100 cents.

random When numbers or objects are chosen at *random*, this means they are chosen without any rule or preference (bias). In a *random* selection process, it is not possible to predict what any particular chosen item will be.

- The winning Lotto numbers must be chosen at *random*, so that no one can cheat. A machine is used to choose the numbers *randomly*, without any person's preference affecting the choice.
- A fair way to decide which learners should do cleaning duty is to write the names of everyone in the class on pieces

of paper and put them in a bag. The teacher can then draw names out of the bag at *random* – no one will be able to affect which name she draws out each time.

See *random sample*

random sample   A *random sample* is a sample chosen from a population in such a way that each member of the population has an equal chance of being chosen.
- To find out whether South Africans prefer to watch soccer or basketball on television, the TV producers asked a *random sample* of 500 people from all over the country which sport they prefer to watch.

See *random*

range (statistical data)   The *range* in a set of statistical data is the number that gives the difference between the highest and lowest values in the set. This is a way of measuring the spread of the data.
- The times of the runners in a half-marathon race are recorded. The fastest time was 72 minutes and the slowest time was 179 minutes. The *range* is 179 – 72 = 107 minutes.

See *data*

range of a function   The *range of a function* is the set of numbers onto which the domain of the function maps. In functions of the form $y = mx + c$ or $y = ax^2 + bx + c$, the x-values form the domain of the function and the y-values form the *range of the function*.
- The function $y = 4x - 6$ maps its domain {2, 3, 4, 5} onto the set {2, 6, 10, 14} which is its *range*.

$$x \rightarrow 4x - 6$$

See *domain; function; mapping*

rate   A *rate* is a comparison of two different kinds of quantities (that is, quantities measured using different kinds of measuring units), using division.
- The distance that a car travels (kilometres) in a given time (hours) is the *rate* that we call its 'speed'. Speed is calculated as kilometres ÷ hours, which is usually written as km/h. A car that travels 200 km in 2 hours is travelling at an average *rate* of $\frac{200}{2} = 100$ km/h.

See *rate of change*

rate of change   A *rate of change* is a comparison of how one kind of quantity changes in relation to another kind of quantity, using division.
- A baby's length is checked every week after birth, and its changing length is recorded on a graph to see if it is growing normally. The *rate of change* of the baby's length week by week is shown by the slope of the graph. The steeper the graph's slope, the faster the *rate of change* of the length.

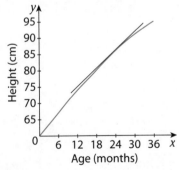

See *rate*

ratio A *ratio* is a comparison of two quantities of the same kind (quantities measured using the same kind of measuring unit), using division.

- In a class of learners with 12 girls and 16 boys, the *ratio* of girls to boys is given as 12 : 16, which can be simplified using division:

$$12 : 16 = \frac{12}{16} = \frac{3}{4}.$$

- The mass of the textbook is 750 g and the mass of the exercise book is 200 g. The *ratio* of their masses is 750 : 200, which can be simplified:

$$750 : 200 = \frac{750}{200} = \frac{75}{20} = \frac{15}{4} = 3\frac{3}{4}.$$

See *simplify*

rational number A *rational number* is any number that can be written in the form $\frac{p}{q}$, where p and q are positive and negative integers and $q \neq 0$. Natural numbers, whole numbers and integers are subsets of the set of *rational numbers* in which $q = 1$.

- Examples of *rational numbers* are:

$$\frac{2}{3}; \frac{3}{5}; \frac{-5}{7}; \frac{49}{-56}; \frac{35}{1}; \frac{-100}{1}; \frac{0}{1}$$

- Any terminating or recurring decimal number can be written as a *rational number*:

$$37{,}2567 = \frac{372\ 567}{10\ 000}$$

$$0{,}131313131313\ldots = \frac{13}{99}$$

See *integer; irrational number; natural number; recurring decimal; whole number*

real number A *real number* is any number which corresponds to a length on the number line. The set of all *real numbers* includes the subsets of all natural numbers, whole numbers, positive and negative integers, rational numbers and irrational numbers.

- Examples of *real numbers* are:
  $3; 8{,}4; -9{,}2; 0; 26{,}98732;$
  $5^{26}; \pi; \sqrt{2}$
- *Real numbers* can be written using decimal notation, whether the decimal terminates, is recurring, or goes on forever without any repeating pattern of digits:

3,245
29,5454545454545454...
812,01001000100001000001...

See *integer; irrational number; natural number; rational number; recurring decimal; whole number*

receive To *receive* something means to get something that another person gives to you. A *receipt* is a document that you get from a person or an organisation, to prove that you have given something to them.

- Every year Nthabiseng *receives* a birthday card from her brother in Zambia.
- The *Receiver of Revenue* is a name for the government department that *receives* all the tax money (revenue) that South Africans pay every month, out of their salaries and wages. When you pay your tax, you get a *receipt* from the tax office to say that they have *received* your money.

reciprocal The *reciprocal* of a number x is the number 1 divided by x. The *reciprocal* of a fraction $\frac{a}{b}$ is $\frac{b}{a}$. Any number multiplied by its *reciprocal* is equal to 1. The *reciprocal* is the multiplicative inverse of the number.

- The *reciprocal* of 4 is $\frac{1}{4}$:

$$4 \times \frac{1}{4} = \frac{4}{1} \times \frac{1}{4} = 1$$

- The *reciprocal* of $\frac{3}{4}$ is $\frac{4}{3}$:

$$\frac{3}{4} \times \frac{4}{3} = 1$$

- The *reciprocal* of 0,2 is 5:

$$0{,}2 = \frac{2}{10} = \frac{1}{5}$$

The *reciprocal* of $\frac{1}{5}$ is $\frac{5}{1}$.

- 0 does not have a *reciprocal*.

See *multiplicative inverse; reciprocal function*

reciprocal function   The function $y = f(x) = \frac{1}{x}$ is called the *reciprocal function*, because it maps every value of x except 0 onto its reciprocal value, $\frac{1}{x}$. The graph of the *reciprocal function* is called a hyperbola.

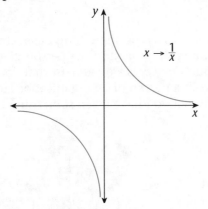

See *function; graph; mapping; reciprocal*

recognise   To *recognise* a thing (or a person) is to know what it is (or who the person is) because you have seen it before.
- You should be able to *recognise* the three different polygons that make up this pattern:

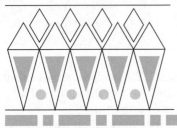

See *polygon*

record   To *record* something means to keep it in a form that will last.
- Storytellers can *record* their stories by writing them on paper, typing them into a computer, or speaking into the microphone of a tape recorder.

- Mathematicians *record* their ideas using mathematical symbols that they write on paper or enter into a computer.

rectangle   A *rectangle* is a quadrilateral with these properties:
- It has two pairs of opposite sides that are equal in length and parallel to each other.
- It has four right angles.
- It has two diagonals that are equal in length and cut each other in half.
- It has two lines of symmetry.

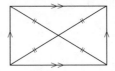

- A square is a type of *rectangle* in which all four sides are the same length.

square

- An oblong is a *rectangle* that is not a square.

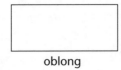

oblong

See *line of symmetry; parallel; quadrilateral; right angle*

rectangle number   A *rectangle number* is a number that can be shown as an array of dots in a rectangular pattern, with more than one row or column. It has at least two factors other than 1, and is therefore never a prime number. Square numbers are one kind of *rectangle number*.

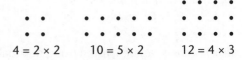

$4 = 2 \times 2$ $10 = 5 \times 2$ $12 = 4 \times 3$

See *prime number; square number*

rectangular prism A *rectangular prism* is a prism whose cross-section is a rectangle. A cuboid is a *rectangular prism*.

See *cross-section; cuboid; prism; rectangle*

recurring decimal A *recurring decimal* is a decimal number in which the pattern of the digits after the decimal comma keeps repeating itself. ('To recur' means 'to keep happening'.) To show that the decimal sequence repeats itself endlessly, a dot is placed over the first and last digit of the recurring sequence.

- A *recurring decimal* may be a single digit:
  - 0,33333333…, which can be written as 0,$\dot{3}$
  - 589,44444444444…, which can be written as 589,$\dot{4}$
- Or it may be a repeating sequence of digits:
  - 0,238238238238238238238238…, which can be written as 0,$\dot{2}3\dot{8}$
  - 1 046,91919191919191…, which can be written as 1 046,$\dot{9}\dot{1}$.
- All *recurring decimals* can be turned into fractions by putting 9s under the recurring digits and treating the result as a fraction:
  - $0,\dot{3} = \frac{3}{9} = \frac{1}{3}$
  - $0,\dot{2}3\dot{8} = \frac{238}{999}$

See *decimal; fraction*

reduce to simplest form To *reduce* a fraction *to its simplest form* means to find the common factors in the numerator and denominator, and cancel these out by dividing them into each other.

- In the fraction $\frac{24}{36}$, 12 is a common factor of 24 and 36. To *reduce* the fraction *to its simplest form*, divide the numerator by 12 and the denominator by 12. This gives $\frac{2}{3}$, the simplest form of this fraction.

See *common factor; fraction*

reflection A *reflection* is a transformation that has the same effect as a mirror. Every point P in front of a mirror (line or plane) maps to an image point P' on the other side of the mirror, so that P and P' are the same distance from the mirror, and the line joining P and P' is at right angles to the mirror. This mirror line is the line of symmetry of the points P and P'.

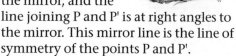

See *line of symmetry; right angle; transformation*

reflex angle A *reflex angle* is an angle that is bigger than 180° and smaller than 360°.

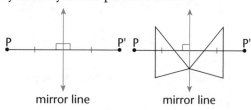

See *acute angle; angle; obtuse angle*

region A *region* is a part of a bigger surface that can be clearly described by referring to its shape, its boundaries, or some other property of the *region*.

- If a circle is drawn on a page, it divides the page surface into two *regions*: the *region* inside the circle (1) and the *region* outside the circle (2).

- The graph of an equation such as $x + y = 6$ divides the plane into two *regions*. These *regions* correspond to the inequalities $x + y > 6$ and $x + y < 6$.

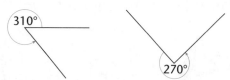

See *circle; graph; inequality; plane*

regular polygon A *regular polygon* is a polygon with all its sides the same length, and all its angles the same size.

- Examples of *regular polygons* are:

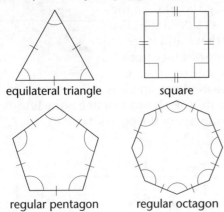

equilateral triangle   square

regular pentagon   regular octagon

See *polygon*

regular polyhedron (plural: polyhedra) A *regular polyhedron* is a three-dimensional shape whose faces are all regular polygons, and whose corners are all the same as each other.

- There are only five *regular polyhedra*:

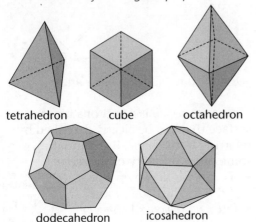

tetrahedron   cube   octahedron

dodecahedron   icosahedron

See *Platonic solids; polygon*

related operations *Related operations* are mathematical operations that are connected to each other.

- Addition and subtraction are *related operations* because subtraction is the inverse of addition:

$$-4 + 4 = 0$$
$$+7 - 7 = 0$$

See *additive inverse*

relation (relationship) A *relation* between two sets of numbers is a way in which they are connected. The *relation* describes a mathematical operation that is done to the one set of numbers, to give the other set of numbers. Functions are one type of *relation*. In everyday English a *relation* is sometimes called a *relationship*.

- There is a *relation* between the following sequences of numbers. The *relation* is described by the equation $y = x^2$.
- In this diagram, the shaded shape S is *related to* the unshaded shape S' by a 90° rotation about the origin.

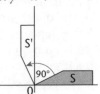

relative frequency The *relative frequency* of an event in statistics is the number of times the event happens in the statistical experiment, divided by the number of trials conducted.

- This graph shows the ages of learners in Grade 10.

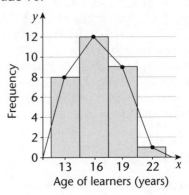

See *event; frequency*

remainder A *remainder* is an amount that is left over when one number is divided into another number. Sometimes the first number divides exactly into the second number and the result is a whole number. But sometimes the division is not exact, and then the answer is a whole number and a *remainder*.

- $49 ÷ 7 = 7$: there is no *remainder*.
- $49 ÷ 5 = 9$ and 4 left over: 4 is the *remainder*.

rent   *Rent* is an amount of money that you pay regularly (every week or every month) to the person who owns the place where you are living, or for the equipment that you are using.
- The Thabane family pays *rent* of R800 per month to the owner of their flat in Hillbrow.
- When Joyce goes to Durban on business she *rents* a car. The car rental costs R120 per day.

repeat, repetition   To *repeat* something means to do it again. *Repetition* means 'doing something again and again'.
- To write a number as the product of its prime factors, start by dividing the number by its lowest prime factor. *Repeat* this operation until all the factors are prime numbers:
  $36 \div 2 = 18$
  $18 \div 2 = 9$
  $9 \div 3 = 3$
  $3 \div 3 = 1$
  So $36 = 2 \times 2 \times 3 \times 3$
- The best way to remember the multiplication tables is through constant *repetition*.

See *prime factors*

repeated addition   *Repeated addition* of whole numbers is another name for multiplication. To multiply a whole number x by a whole number y is the same as adding x to itself repeatedly, y times.
- $12 \times 4 = 12 + 12 + 12 + 12 = 48$

repeated subtraction   *Repeated subtraction* of whole numbers is another name for division. Subtracting a whole number x from a whole number y, z times is the same as saying $y \div x = z$.
- $20 \div 4 = 5$. This can be written as a *repeated subtraction*:
  $20 - 5 - 5 - 5 - 5 = 0$

replace   To *replace* something means to take it away and put something else in its place.
- *Replace* the variable x in the equation with a number that makes the equation true:
  $31 + x = 45$ $(31 + 14 = 45)$

represent   To *represent* something (such as an idea, a shape, a number, etc.) means to show that thing using a symbol, a diagram, a drawing or some other form.
- The set of x-values $\{3, 6, 9, 12\}$ maps onto the set of y-values $\{9, 36, 81, 144\}$, for the function $y = x^2$. *Represent* this on a graph.

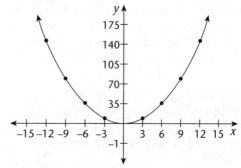

- The results of a survey show that, in a class of 25 learners:
  ‣ 4 learners speak English at home
  ‣ 9 learners speak isiZulu at home
  ‣ 7 learners speak Sesotho at home
  ‣ 5 learners speak Afrikaans at home.
  Represent these results on a bar graph.

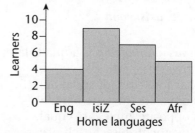

result   A *result* is the solution to a problem, such as a value obtained by mathematical calculation.
- The *result* of the calculation:
  $$\frac{(35 + (4 \times 21) - 15)}{2} \text{ is 52.}$$

See *answer*

reverse order   To arrange a group of items in *reverse order* means to arrange them starting with the last item in the group and ending with the first item.
• If we rewrite the list of numbers 12, 14, 16, 18, 20 in *reverse order*, we get the list 20, 18, 16, 14, 12.

revision   *Revision* is the work that learners do when they go back to study all their school subjects for that year again, to prepare for a test or an exam.
• There is a *revision* section at the end of every module in the textbook to help you go over everything you have learnt in the module and practise your skills.
• In the last two weeks before the exams, the learners go to *revision* classes, where they go over all the mathematics they have learnt during the year.

revolution, revolve   A *revolution* is a complete turn about a point or an axis, so that you arrive back at your starting point. The angle size of a *revolution* is 360°.
To *revolve* means to travel around a point or an object in a complete circle or ellipse path.
• It takes one year for the Earth to *revolve* around the Sun. The Earth *revolves* around its own axis every 24 hours.

See *angle; axis; point*

rhombus   A *rhombus* is a quadrilateral with these properties:
• It has four sides of equal length.
• Its opposite sides are parallel.
• Its opposite angles are equal.
• Its diagonals bisect each other at right angles.
• Its diagonals bisect the interior angles.
• Its diagonals are lines of symmetry.
A square is a special type of *rhombus* in which all the angles are equal to 90°.

• A *rhombus* is often described as a diamond shape, because of the way it looks when it stands on one end.

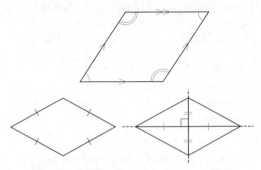

See *diagonal; line of symmetry; parallel; quadrilateral; right angle*

right, right angle, right-angled triangle, right cone or pyramid, right prism   In everyday English *right* means 'correct' or 'true'. In mathematics, *right* is used to describe shapes with special properties.
• A *right angle* is an angle of size 90°.

right angle

• A *right-angled triangle* is a triangle in which one angle is a *right angle*.

right-angled triangle

• A *right cone or pyramid* is a cone or pyramid whose vertex V is directly above the centre of its base. If the vertex is not directly above the centre of the base, it is an oblique cone or pyramid.

right pyramid   right cone   oblique pyramid

- A *right prism* is a prism whose sides are at *right angles* to its ends. If the sides are not at *right angles* to the ends, it is an oblique prism.

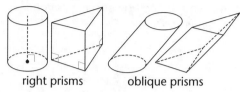

right prisms   oblique prisms

See *angle; cone; oblique; prism; pyramid; vertex*

right side   The *right side* of a shape or object is the side to the east, if the shape or object is facing north. The right side is opposite the left side of the shape or object.
- If you are facing Table Mountain, the District Six Hotel is on the *right side* of the street.
- The map of Africa shows the Indian Ocean on the *right side* (the east coast) of the country, and the Atlantic Ocean on the *left side* (the west coast).

See *left*

Roman numerals   *Roman numerals* are the symbols that were used by the ancient Romans to represent numbers. These numerals are often used today to number the pages of books, or items in a list, or the hours on a clock face.
The symbols have two forms, capital numerals and small numerals:
    I i = 1
    V v = 5
    X x = 10
    L l = 50
    C c = 100
    D d = 500
    M m = 1 000

The numerals are repeated and combined to give different number values.
The order of the numerals shows whether they are to be added or subtracted. The Romans did not use a place value system.

(See the table on page 149 of this dictionary.)
See *numeral; place value*

root of an equation   A *root of an equation* is any number that satisfies the equation (makes it true). It is a value of the variable that gives a solution to the equation. Some equations have only one root; other equations have two or more roots.
- The *root of the equation* $3x - 1 = 5$ is 2, because if the variable x is 2, then $3x - 1 = 5$ is $(3 \times 2) - 1 = 5$, which is true.
- Quadratic equations can have one, two or no roots. The *roots of the equation* $x^2 - 3x + 2 = 0$ are 2 and 1:
  $(2)^2 - (3 \times 2) + 2 = 0$
  so $x = 2$ satisfies the equation.
  $(1)^2 - (3 \times 1) + 2 = 0$
  so $x = 1$ also satisfies the equation.

See *equation; quadratic equation; variable*

rotate   To *rotate* means to turn.
- The triangle ABC is *rotated* through 90° to give the triangle A'B'C'.

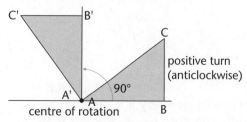

positive turn (anticlockwise)

centre of rotation

See *rotation; transformation*

rotation   A *rotation* is a transformation that moves points so that they stay the same distance from a fixed point, which is called the centre of *rotation*. The points are all turned through the same angle about the centre, and they seem to move along arcs of concentric circles.

A *rotation* is defined when its centre, the angle of *rotation*, and the direction of the turn are given. An anticlockwise turn is called a positive turn, and a clockwise turn is called a negative turn.

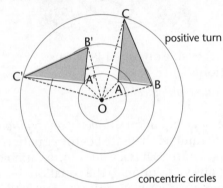

concentric circles

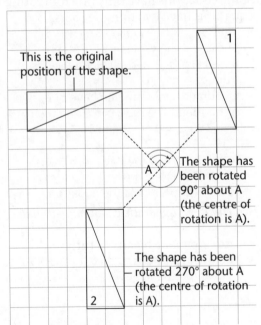

This is the original position of the shape.

The shape has been rotated 90° about A (the centre of rotation is A).

The shape has been rotated 270° about A (the centre of rotation is A).

See *transformation*

rotational symmetry   A shape has *rotational symmetry* if it can be mapped onto itself by a rotation of less than 360°.

- A flower with five petals can be rotated about its centre to map onto itself through an angle that is $\frac{1}{5}$ of a turn (that is $\frac{1}{5} \times 360° = 72°$) and any multiple of this angle. The flower has *rotational symmetry* of order 5.

- A hexagonal box of chocolates can be rotated about its main axis through an angle that is $\frac{1}{6}$ of a turn ($\frac{1}{6} \times 360 = 60°$) and any multiple of this angle, so it has *rotational symmetry* of order 6 about this axis.

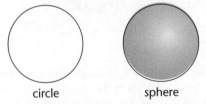

See *axis; symmetry*

round   1. A shape constructed from curves, like a circle or sphere, is *round*. 2. A *round* number is a number that has been rounded off to the nearest multiple of 10 – tens, hundreds, thousands, etc.

circle   sphere

- These are examples of round numbers:
  30   450   700   5 000

See *circle; round off; sphere*

rounding error   A *rounding error* is the difference between the exact value of a number and the value of the number after it has been rounded off.

- When 362,82518 is rounded off to 362,83, the *rounding error* is
  362,82518 – 362,83 = – 0,00482.

See *round off*

round off (rounding)   To *round off* a number means to give an approximately equal number that is a round number. To do this, we follow the rules for *rounding off* numbers:

- If the last numeral in the number is 5 or more than 5, round up to the next round number.
- If the last numeral in the number is less than 5, round down to the previous round number.

Numbers can be *rounded off* to the nearest 10, 100, 1 000 or any other suitable round number. Numbers can also be *rounded off* to a particular decimal place, following the same rules.

- 37 *rounded off* to the nearest 10 is 40.
- 64 *rounded off* to the nearest 10 is 60.
- 64 *rounded off* to the nearest 100 is 100.
- 5 350 *rounded off* to the nearest hundred is 5 400.
- 362,82518 *rounded off* to three decimal places is 362,825.
- 362,82518 *rounded off* to two decimal places is 362,83.
- 362,82518 *rounded off* to no decimal places is 363.

See *decimal places*

row   A *row* is a horizontal arrangement of numbers, words or shapes (from left to right on the page).

- There are three *rows* in this table.

Row 1			
Row 2			
Row 3			

See *column; horizontal; table (data)*

rule   1. A *rule* is a fixed way of doing a task, always using the same steps or method.
2. A ruler is sometimes called a *rule*.

- The *rule* for doing arithmetic calculations is to do the operations in this order: brackets, of, divide, multiply, add, subtract. This rule is sometimes called the BODMAS *rule*.

See *BODMAS*

S

salary   A *salary* is a fixed monthly payment that a worker (employee) earns. See *daily wage*

sample   1. In everyday language, a *sample* is a small amount or a piece of a bigger item that you try out before buying the big item.
2. In statistics, a *sample* is a small group of people whom you question about a topic, to find out what a much bigger group of people thinks about the topic. The *sample* of people is chosen so that it represents the bigger group fairly.

- The supermarket is giving customers free *samples* of a new type of bread to taste. They hope this will make the customers want to buy the bread.
- To find out whether South Africans want to be the hosts of the 2010 World Cup, a *sample* of 1 000 people was asked for their views. This *sample* was used to decide what the whole population of South Africa thinks about hosting the World Cup.

scalar quantity   A *scalar quantity* is a quantity that has size but no direction.

- Speed is a *scalar quantity* – it describes how fast an object is travelling, but not the direction in which it is going. Other examples of *scalar quantities* are temperature and air pressure.

See *speed*

scale   A *scale* is an instrument for measuring mass.

- There are different kinds of *scales*:

See *mass*

scale factor   A *scale factor* is a ratio that you use to make a drawing of a shape smaller or larger. It is used when drawing a map of a place, or making a model of a life-size object. Using a *scale factor* means that every part of the drawing has the same relative size as the relative sizes of the objects or places in real life.

• To draw a map of a whole country on one sheet of paper, a *scale factor* must be used to reduce the size of the country to the size of the paper. For example, let 1 centimetre on the drawing be equal to 100 kilometres (1 000 000 centimetres) of real distance on the land.

• The *scale factor* for this map is written as the ratio 1 : 20 000 000.

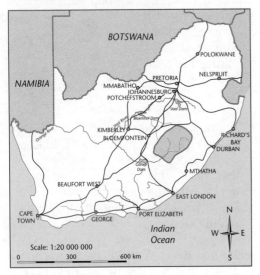

See *factor; scale plan*

scale plan   A *scale plan* is a plan or diagram of a real place or a real object, in which the real thing is reduced in size by means of a scale factor.

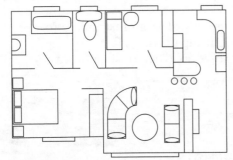

See *scale factor*

scalene triangle   A *scalene triangle* is a triangle with three sides all of different lengths, and three angles all of different sizes.

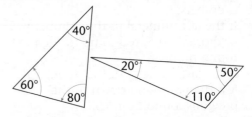

See *equilateral triangle; isosceles triangle*

scatter diagram   A *scatter diagram* is a diagram used in statistics to compare two variables and show the strength of the relationship (correlation) between them. The set of values of the two variables is plotted as points on the diagram. You can then compare the positions of the points to see how they are scattered.

• This *scatter diagram* shows the height and shoe size of each person in a group as a point on the graph. Because a person's shoe size usually increases as their height increases, the points on the diagram all lie close to the same diagonal line on the graph, called the 'line of best fit', and have a high correlation.

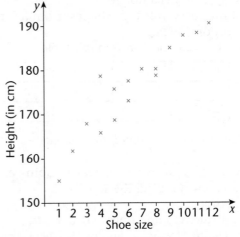

See *graph*

schedule   A *schedule* is a timetable that sets out what tasks must be done at different times. A *schedule* can also be any list that shows how people's activities are organised.

- The nurses look at the *schedule* every day to see what they must do for each patient.
- According to this *schedule*, the farm delivery truck must make three stops to deliver apples to farm stalls in Grabouw, Elgin and Franschhoek.

DELIVERY ROSTER				
STOPS	TIME IN	TIME OUT	NO. OF CRATES	DATE
1. GRABOUW FARMSTALL	8.00 a.m.	8.30 a.m.	7	03/07
2. ELGIN OASIS	9.00 a.m.	9.30 a.m.	5	03/07
3. FRANSCHHOEK ROADSIDE DELI	12.15 a.m.	12.45 a.m.	9	03/07

scientific calculator   A *scientific calculator* is a calculator that is programmed to do the kinds of calculations used in advanced mathematics. These calculations are often used in scientific experiments.

See *calculator*

scientific notation   *Scientific notation* is a method of writing numbers. A number is in *scientific notation* if it is written as a number between 1 and 10, multiplied by a power of 10.
- 233 can be written in *scientific notation* as $2{,}33 \times 10^2$.
- 180 000 000 can be written in *scientific notation* as $1{,}8 \times 10^8$.

See *power of a number; standard (index) form*

second (position)   The *second* position is the position that comes just after the first position.
- Ayanda is in the *second* position in the queue.
- The *second* item on the list is 'potatoes'.

See *first*

second (unit of angle size)   A *second* is a unit for measuring very small angle sizes. We usually measure angles in degrees. One degree is divided into 60 minutes, and one 1 minute is divided into 60 *seconds*. So one degree is equal to 3 600 *seconds*. The symbol for seconds is ".

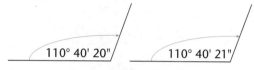

See *angle; degree*

second (unit of time)   A *second* is a small unit of time. There are 60 *seconds* in 1 minute, and 60 minutes in 1 hour. So there are 3 600 *seconds* in 1 hour.
- One *second* is the time it takes a world-class sprinter to run 10 metres.
- A *second* is about the time it takes for your heart to beat once.

See *hour; minute (time)*

second hand   The *second hand* on an analogue clock face is the hand that shows how many seconds have passed. It takes 60 seconds for the hand to move around the clock face once.

See *clock face; minute hand*

sector of a circle   A *sector of a circle* is a region of a circle formed by two radii and it is part of the circle's circumference. The smaller region formed is called the minor sector. The larger region formed is called the major sector.

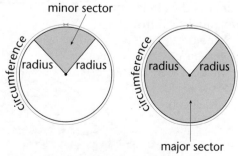

See *circle; circumference; radius*

segment of a circle   A *segment of a circle* is a region of a circle formed when a straight line is drawn to join two points on the circumference. The line divides the circle into two parts: a smaller part called the minor segment, and a larger part called the major segment.

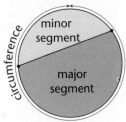

See *circle; circumference*

self-inverse   An element is *self-inverse* if it combines with itself to produce the identity element.
- 1 is *self-inverse* because $1 \times 1 = 1$.
- -1 is *self-inverse* because $-1 \times -1 = 1$.

sell   To *sell* something means to give it to someone in exchange for money.
- Thembisa *sells* sunglasses at the market. People pay her R25 for each pair of sunglasses.

See *buy*

selling price   The *selling price* of an item is the price that it sells for in a shop.
- The *selling price* of a new computer is between about R5 999 and R8 999.

See *cost price*

semi-circle   A *semi-circle* is one half of a circle. 'Semi-' means 'half'.
A *semi-circle* is formed by any diameter of a circle that cuts the circle into two equal sections.

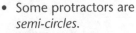

- Some protractors are *semi-circles*.
- The goal scoring areas on hockey fields and netball courts are *semi-circles*.

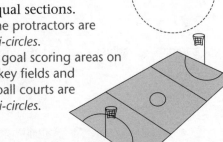

See *circle; diameter; half*

sentence   A *sentence* is a group of words that expresses a complete thought.
A *sentence* starts with a capital letter and ends with a full stop.
- These are examples of *sentences*:
  - My cat's name is Fred.
  - Tomorrow I'm going to start studying for my mathematics test, then I'm going to play soccer, and then I'm going to visit my friend to watch TV.
  - Yes.

separate   Two or more shapes, objects or groups are *separate* if they do not touch each other in any way, are not combined into one group, and if the one is not inside the other.
- There are three *separate* groups of people:
  - people aged below 25
  - people aged 26–40
  - people aged 50–75.

- There are four *separate* triangles in the frame below.

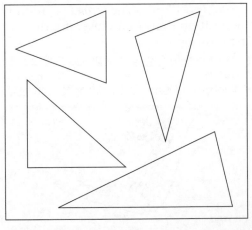

sequence   A *sequence* is a set of numbers in a particular order. It is normally defined by some rule so that a formula can be given that describes any number in the *sequence*. Each number in the *sequence* is called a term of the *sequence*.
- Examples of *sequences*:
  5, 8, 11, 14, 17, …, $3n + 2$, …
  The rule for finding the number in the nth position (the nth term) in this *sequence* is $3n + 2$. The number in the 5th position is therefore $(3 \times 5) + 2 = 17$.
- 6, 9, 14, 21, 30, …, $n^2 + 5$, …
  The rule for finding the nth term in this *sequence* is $n^2 + 5$. The number in the 4th position (the 4th term) is therefore $4^2 + 5 = 16 + 5 = 21$.

See *formula; series*

series   A *series* is the sum of the numbers in a sequence. A *series* can be calculated by adding any given number of terms in the sequence.
- The *series* $1 + 3 + 5 + 7 + 9 + 11 + 13 + 15 + 17 + 19$ is formed by adding the first ten odd numbers. Its sum is 100.
- The *series* $5 + 8 + 11 + 14 + 17$ is formed by adding the first five terms in the sequence 5, 8, 11, 14, 17, …, $3n + 2$, … . The sum of this *series* is 55.

See *sequence*

service fee   A *service fee* is an amount of money that the bank charges the customer for the services it offers.
- When you deposit money into your savings account, the bank charges you a *service fee*. They say this fee is to pay for the work they must do to handle your money and keep it safe from thieves.

set   A *set* is a collection of objects, called the members or elements of the *set*. To show that the objects belong to the same *set*, they are put between curly brackets { }. A *set* can be finite or infinite. *Sets* are often labelled with a single letter. The symbol ∈ is used to show that an object is a member of a *set*, and ∉ is used to show that it is not a member.

- The *set* of prime numbers less than twelve is given as {2, 3, 5, 7, 11}. This *set* can be labelled with any letter, for example C = {2, 3, 5, 7, 11}. $7 \in C$, but $15 \notin C$.
- The *set* of months of the year beginning with J is given as {January, June, July}.
- The *set* F = {multiples of 5} is an infinite *set*.
- The *set* G = {multiples of 5 between 6 and 32} is a finite *set*.

See *element of a set; finite; infinite set; subset*

set square   A *set square* is a drawing tool. It is used to draw accurate angles and straight lines on diagrams of shapes such as buildings and machine parts. It is a triangular piece of wood, plastic or metal with angles of 90° and 45° and 45°, or 90° and 30° and 60°.

See *angle; triangle*

several   *Several* means 'a few', more than two objects but not very many. It is used to describe a small number of objects that do not need to be counted accurately.
- There are *several* people waiting for the taxi.

shape   A *shape* is the way an object looks, its outline or form. In mathematics, a *shape* can be described in terms of the size of its lines, curves and angles.
- There are hats of all *shapes* and sizes on sale.
- These are examples of mathematical *shapes*:

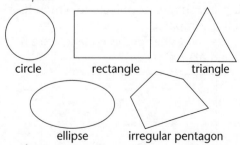

circle   rectangle   triangle

ellipse   irregular pentagon

share To *share* something means to divide it into parts. The parts can then be given to different people, or placed in different groups. To *share* can also mean to allow many people to all use the same object.
- One large pizza is big enough for the whole family to *share*.
- The sweets were *shared* out among the whole class. Each learner received three sweets from the bag.
- The football players, dog walkers, joggers and lazy people all *share* the same park.

shares A business can sell *shares* in its capital stock (its value) to people who do not work for the company. The money that these people pay for the *shares* is used to help the business expand (get bigger).

shibiri The *shibiri* is a unit of length that is used in Ethiopia and other parts of east Africa. One *shibiri* is the distance from the tip of your little finger to the tip of your thumb. In English, the word 'span' means the same thing.

short, shorter than The *short* side of a shape is the side that has the smaller length. A *short* shape or object is one whose length is smaller than the length of other shapes or objects to which it is being compared.
- The *short* sides of this rectangle are BC and AD.

- The distance from Polokwane to Tshwane is *shorter than* the distance from Tshwane to East London.

short hand (clock) The *short hand* on a clock face shows the hour. It takes 60 minutes for the *short hand* to move from one hour to the next on the clock face.
See *clock face; long hand*

short method A *short method* is a quicker way of doing a calculation or solving a problem.
- Multiplication is a *short method* for adding the same number many times – if you know your multiplication tables!
See *multiplication table*

SI units *SI units* are the scientific measuring units that make up the Système International – the international measuring system that is used in most parts of the world for mathematical and scientific work.
- The measuring units in the metric system are all *SI units*. (Refer to the table page 151–3 of this dictionary.)
See *metric system; standard unit of measurement*

side A *side* is a line segment or a surface that forms a boundary (edge) of a shape.
- The three *sides* of this triangle are the line segments OP, PQ and QO.

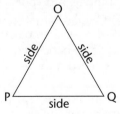

- The *sides* AB and AC form the angle BAC.

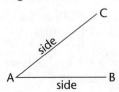

- This cuboid has six *sides*.

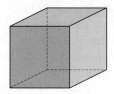

See *line segment; shape*

sign   A *sign* is any symbol or picture that is used to express an instruction or some information, in a short way.
- The *sign* × means 'multiply'.
- The *sign* ☠ means 'This substance is poisonous – beware!'
- The *sign* ✈ means 'This is the road to the airport.'

significant figures   'Significant' means 'important' and 'figures' here refers to the digits in a number. The most *significant figure* in a number is the first non-zero digit starting from the left, because it tells you the most about the total value of the number. The answers to numerical calculations are sometimes rounded off to a given number of *significant figures*.
- In the number 238,95, although the left-hand digit is only 2 it represents 200, while the largest digit, 9, only represents 9 tenths. 2 is the most *significant figure* in this number. The next most *significant figure* is 3, which represents 30. The least *significant figure* is the 5, because it represents the smallest part of the number, 5 hundredths.
- Examples of numbers rounded to different *significant figures*:
  ‣ 9,434285 rounded to four *significant figures* is 9,434
  ‣ 546,3287 rounded to three *significant figures* is 546
  ‣ 0,49012 rounded to three *significant figures* is 0,490
  ‣ 0,002054 rounded to two *significant figures* is 0,0021.

See *digit; round off*

similar   In geometry, two shapes are *similar* if they are the same in every way except size.
Similar shapes have corresponding angles that are equal, and lines that are in proportion.
Similar shapes can be turned (this is called rotation), flipped (reflection) or made to slide along a line (translation).
- These shapes are all *similar*.

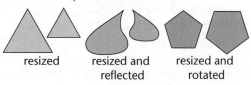

resized   resized and   resized and
             reflected   rotated

similar figures   *Similar figures* are figures (shapes or objects) that have the same shape but different sizes. Similar polygons are equi-angular (they have the same angles) but different side lengths. The lengths of their corresponding sides are in proportion.
- Paper is sold in different sizes – A1 sheets, A2 sheets, A3 sheets, A4 sheets and A5 sheets. Each size is half the size of the one before it, but all the paper sizes have the same shape. They are *similar figures*.

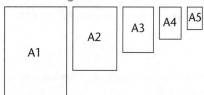

- Two quadrilaterals ABCD and PQRS are *similar figures* when the angles that correspond to one another are equal: ∠A = ∠P, ∠B = ∠Q, ∠C = ∠R, ∠D = ∠S and the ratios of the lengths of the corresponding sides are also equal. In this example PQ : AB = QR : BC = RS : CD = SP : DA = 2 : 1

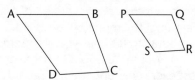

The linear scale factor in this example is 2.

See *linear scale factor; polygon*

simple   An activity is *simple* when it is easy to do, or has only a few steps or parts.
- These arithmetic calculations are *simple*: you can do them in your head and without a calculator.
  2 + 5
  12 × 10
  100 + 200 + 500
- This is a *simple* diagram. It only has three elements: two parallel lines and one transversal.

simple closed curve   A *simple closed curve* is any curve that divides a surface into only two regions – a region inside the curve and a region outside the curve.
- These are all examples of *simple closed curves*:

See *curve*

simple fraction   A *simple fraction* is a fraction that has a numerator and a denominator which are both whole numbers.
- These are some examples of *simple fractions*:
  $\dfrac{3}{8}$ $\dfrac{100}{123}$ $\dfrac{44}{579}$

See *denominator; fraction; numerator; whole number*

simple interest   When a person is paid interest at regular intervals on a sum of money that has been invested or loaned to someone, without the interest being added to the sum invested, the interest earned is called *simple interest*.
- Thabang borrowed R500 from Lesego and agreed to pay *simple interest* of 5% per year until the money was repaid. This amounts to R25 per year in interest. Thabang will pay Lesego R25 per year in interest every year until he has repaid the R500 loan.

See *compound interest; interest*

simplest form   A fraction is written in its *simplest form* when both the numerator and the denominator are as small as possible. To simplify a fraction, you cancel out the common factors from the numerator and the denominator.
- The fraction $\frac{12}{20}$ can be written as a *simple fraction* by cancelling the numerator and denominator:
  $\dfrac{^{3}\cancel{12}}{\cancel{20}_{5}} = \dfrac{3}{5}$

See *cancel; denominator; fraction; numerator*

simplify   To *simplify* something means to make it simpler.
- To *simplify* an arithmetic problem, you calculate the answer:
  $13 \times 25 + 56 \div 7 = 325 + 8 = 333$
- To *simplify* an algebraic expression, you group the like terms:
  $2(x + 3y) = 3(4x - y)$
  $= 2x + 6y + 12x - 3y = 14x + 3y$
- To *simplify* a fraction, you write the fraction in its simplest form:
  $\dfrac{125}{500} = \dfrac{25}{100} = \dfrac{5}{20} = \dfrac{1}{4}$

See *algebraic expression; simplest form*

simultaneous equations   'Simultaneous' means 'at the same time'. When a problem involves two variables, and they are related by two equations, then the equations have to be solved together (simultaneously). This can be done by drawing graphs of the two equations, or by using algebraic methods to combine and solve the equations.
- Suppose you need to find the values of x and y so that:
  $2x + y = 7$ and $x - y = 8$
  Add the two equations together:
  $2x + y = 7$
  $x - y = 8$
  $3x + 0 = 15$ so $x = 5$
  Substitute 5 for x in the first equation gives $y = -3$
  So the solution that satisfies both equations is the ordered pair $(x; y) = (5; -3)$.

If you draw the graphs of both equations, they intersect at the point whose coordinates are $(x; y) = (5; -3)$. This is another way to find the values of x and y that satisfy both equations.

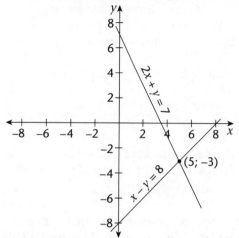

See *equation; variable*

single figures   The numbers from 0 to 9 are sometimes called *single figures*, because each of these numbers is written with only one digit: 0, 1, 2, 3, 4, 5, 6, 7, 8, 9

See *digit*

size   The *size* of a shape or object is how big it is. *Size* is described by giving the measurements of the shape or object – its length, height, mass, volume, or other relevant measurements.

- The *size* of your shoes should match the *size* of your feet, or else you will find it hard to walk properly.

See *height; length; mass; volume*

sketch   A *sketch* is a rough drawing of something, without any accurate measurements or shapes.

- It is helpful to draw a *sketch* of a geometry problem while you are trying to solve it. On the *sketch* you can write in each measurement as you work it out.

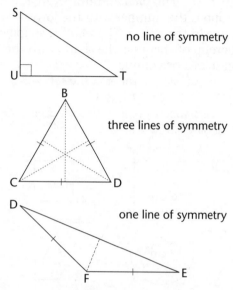

no line of symmetry

three lines of symmetry

one line of symmetry

slant height   *Slant height* is the distance along the surface of a cone from the vertex to the base. The *slant height l* is used to calculated the area A of the curved surface of the cone.

- $A = \pi(r + l)$

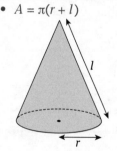

small   1. A *small* shape or object is thin and narrow and takes up very little space.
2. A *small* number is a number with very low value.

See *large*

smaller than   A number is *smaller than* another number if it has a lower value.

- 6 is *smaller than* 7.

    −12 is *smaller than* −5.

    $\frac{3}{100}$ is *smaller than* $\frac{1}{10}$.

smallest   The *smallest* number in a group is the number with the lowest value in the group. The *smallest* shape in a group of shapes is the shape with the least area or volume.

- The *smallest* number in the set A = {3, 5, 80, 114} is 3.
- The *smallest* shape in this group is square ABCD with area 4 cm².

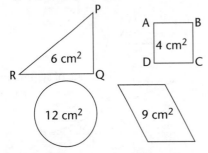

See *area; volume*

solid   A *solid* is a shape that has three dimensions – length, breadth and height. Most *solids* have flat sides called faces; the faces meet at edges. Some *solids* have curved surfaces that form a continuous face.

- All polyhedra are *solids*.

- A sphere is a *solid* with one continuous curved face.

- A cylinder is a *solid* with one curved face and two flat faces.

See *dimension; edge; face; polyhedron; sphere*

solution   A *solution* is a way of reasoning, step-by-step, that gives the answer to a mathematical problem. The final answer to the problem is also called the *solution*.

- The *solution* to the equation:
    $3(x - 4) = x - 6$ is the step-by-step reasoning that gives the value of x that satisfies this equation.
    $3(x - 4) = x - 6$
    Multiplying out the bracket gives
    $3x - 12 = x - 6$.
    Adding 12 to both sides gives $3x = x + 6$.
    Taking away x from both sides gives
    $2x = 6$.
    Dividing both sides by 2 gives $x = 3$.
    So the *solution* of the equation is $x = 3$.

See *equation; solve*

solution set   Sometimes a problem has more than one answer (solution). The set of all the different answers to the problem is called the *solution set* for the problem.

- There are three different solutions to the equation $(x^2 - 4)(x - 3) = 0$.
    $x = 2$, $x = -2$ and $x = 3$ each satisfy the equation.
    So the *solution set* for the equation $(x^2 - 4)(x - 3) = 0$ is {2, −2, 3}.

See *equation; set; solution*

solve   To *solve* a problem means to find the solution (answer) to the problem.

- To *solve* the equation $2x + 3 = 7$ means to find the number that makes the equation true.
- To *solve* the following problem means to find the answer to the question:
    If it takes 5 people 1 hour to dig a hole 6 m deep, how many hours will it take 1 person to dig the same hole?

See *equation; solution*

sort   To *sort* a group of items means to arrange the items in the group according to a given rule or method.

- Sedick is *sorting* the T-shirts according to their sizes, S, M, L and XL.

- *Sort* the following numbers into sets of odd and even numbers: 23, 30, 66, 67, 91, 205, 1 008.
  Solution:
  odd numbers = {23, 67, 91, 205}
  even numbers = {30, 66, 1 008}

south   *South* is one of the four cardinal (main) points on the compass. It is the direction opposite north on the compass.

special numbers   0 and 1 are *special numbers* and have particular properties as illustrated in the entry under 'identity element'.

specific   To *specify* something means to say exactly which item in a group you are talking about, or using. A *specific* item is one particular item that you choose from a group. A *specific* order of items is a way of arranging the items that obeys a particular rule.

- My father likes all kinds of music, but my mother likes only one *specific* kind – R&B.

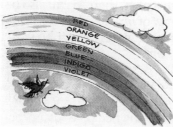

- Choose the *specific* number from the set {3, 4, 5, 6} that satisfies each of these equations:
  $3 + \square = 6$
  $3 - \square = -1$
  $3 \times \square = 18$
  $3 + 5 + \square = 13$
- The colours of the rainbow are arranged in a *specific* order according to the wavelength of each colour – they go from the longest to the shortest wavelength: red, orange, yellow, green, blue, indigo, violet.

speculate   To *speculate* means to guess what the possible solutions to a problem could be, using whatever knowledge you have about the problem. Scientists often start working on a problem by *speculating* about possible solutions, before they begin doing the experiments that will help them to understand and solve the problem.

- It is too soon to know which team will win the next football World Cup. All we can do is *speculate* that it could be Brazil, or Cameroon, or Germany.

speed   The *speed* of an object is a measure of how fast it is moving. *Speed* is given as the distance an object will travel in a unit of time (such as a second, minute, hour, etc.).

- A car that travels 18 km in 15 minutes, at a constant *speed*, has a *speed* of 72 kilometres per hour (km/h).
- Light travels at a *speed* of 300 000 kilometres per second (km/s).

See *distance*

speedometer   A *speedometer* is an instrument for measuring the speed of a moving object.

- The *speedometer* on a car's dashboard shows how fast the car is travelling, in kilometres per hour.

See *speed*

sphere   A *sphere* is a perfectly round shape. It is defined as the set of points P in space that are all the same distance *r* from a fixed point O. O is the centre of the sphere and *r* is its radius.

- Examples of a *sphere* are a ball or a soap bubble.

See *centre of a circle; radius*

spherical   A *spherical* object is an object in the shape of a sphere.

- Balls and bubbles are *spherical* objects.

spiral A spiral is a flat (two-dimensional) curve that starts at a point and moves in ever-widening circular arcs around that point. A three-dimensional *spiral* is called a helix: it is a curve that moves around a central point and also up above that point.

- The seeds in a sunflower are arranged in a *spiral* pattern.
- A three-dimensional *spiral* (helix) can be seen in the thread of a screw, the path of a *spiral* staircase, the shape of some sea shells, the spring of a watch, the patterns of seeds in a pine cone and a *spiral* telephone cord.

See *curve*

square (shape) A *square* is a regular quadrilateral. All its sides are of equal length and all its angles are right angles. Its diagonals are equal in length. They bisect each other and intersect at right angles. A *square* has 4 lines of symmetry. The opposite sides of a *square* are parallel.

diagonals bisect each   4 lines of
other at right angles   symmetry

- The *square* shape is used in many patterns because it is so symmetrical. Wall and floor tiles are often *squares*.

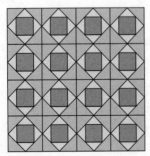

See *diagonal; line of symmetry; parallel; quadrilateral; right angle*

square brackets *Square brackets* are the brackets [ ] that are sometimes used in printed texts.

square net A *square net* is a net that consists of square shapes.

- The net of a cube is a *square net*:

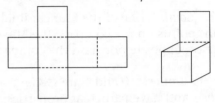

See *cube; net; square (shape)*

square number, square a number A *square number* is any number x multiplied by itself, that is, any number x to the power of 2: $x \times x = x^2$. To *square a number* means to multiply the number by itself. The term 'square' comes from the fact that any number to the power of 2 can be shown as dots arranged in a square pattern.

- Some *square numbers*:
  $1 = 1 \times 1 = 1^2$
  $4 = 2 \times 2 = 2^2$
  $9 = 3 \times 3 = 3^2$
  $16 = 4 \times 4 = 4^2$
  $25 = 5 \times 5 = 5^2$
  $56\ 169 = 237 \times 237 = 237^2$

  1   4   9   16   25

See *power of a number; square (shape)*

square root The *square root* of a number m is the number n which, when multiplied by itself, gives m: $n \times n = n^2 = m$. If n is the *square root* of m, then $-n$ will also be a *square root* of m: $-n \times -n = (-n)^2 = m$. The *square root* of m can be written with the symbol $\sqrt{m}$.

- 3 is the positive *square root* of 9 because $3 \times 3 = 9$.
  This can be written as $\sqrt{9} = +3$.
- −3 is also the negative *square root* of 9 because $-3 \times -3 = 9$.

See *square number*

square unit (square millimetre, square centimetre, square metre, square kilometre)   *Square units* are the measuring units used to measure the surface area of a shape. They are called '*square*' *units* because each unit is a square of length 1 unit and breadth 1 unit: the area of the unit is equal to length × breadth = 1 unit × 1 unit = $(1 \text{ unit})^2$.

The *square units* commonly used to measure areas of different sizes are:
- square millimetres (mm^2)
- square centimetres (cm^2)
- square metres (m^2)
- square kilometres (km^2).

The area of any shape can be described by calculating how many mm^2, cm^2, m^2 or km^2 will fit into the shape.
- The area of a piece of A4 paper is 623,7 cm^2.
- $3 \times 9 = 27$ square units
  ∴ area = 27 square units

See *area*

standard (index) form   *Standard (index) form* is another name for scientific notation. A number is expressed in *standard form* when it is given as a number with one non-zero digit to the left of the decimal comma, multiplied by a power of 10. All numbers can be expressed in this way. *Standard form* is very useful for writing very large or very small numbers.
- Some numbers expressed in *standard (index) form*:
  $329 = 3,29 \times 10^2$
  $46\ 700 = 4,67 \times 10^4$
  $0,0071 = 7,1 \times 10^{-3}$
- When the result of a calculation with a calculator is too big for the calculator display panel, it is presented in *standard form*. For example, when the calculation 865^3 is done on a calculator the result is shown on the display as:

  6.4721463^{08}

  which equals 647 214 630.

- A molecule of water has a mass of $2,99 \times 10^{-26}$ kg.
- The mass of the moon is $7,37 \times 10^{22}$ kg.

See *scientific notation*

standard unit of measurement
A *standard unit of measurement* is a measuring unit that is used in a system such as the metric system or the imperial system. The measuring units are standard because they do not change from one place to another. For example, a kilometre in Egypt is the same length as a kilometre in South Africa and a kilometre in Brazil. Measuring instruments such as scales, rulers and measuring jugs are all marked with *standard units of measurement*. (Refer to the table on page 151–3 of this dictionary.)
- The metric system is also called the SI (Système International) because it is now the main measuring system used around the world, and the metric units are *standard units of measurement* in many countries. The *standard* metric *units of measurement* such as centimetres, kilograms, litres, etc. are sometimes called SI units. Standard units in the imperial system are units such as feet, inches, miles, pounds and gallons.

See *imperial units; metric system; SI units*

statistics   *Statistics* is the branch of mathematics that concerns the collection, interpretation and analysis of certain kinds of information called data. The mathematicians who do this kind of work are called statisticians.
- *Statistics* is a useful mathematical tool for understanding many aspects of our lives. Some of the questions that can be explored using *statistics* are:
  ‣ Is Earth getting hotter or colder?
  ‣ Do more girls than boys pass the matric exam?
  ‣ Which are the main home languages in South Africa?
  ‣ What kinds of food do people like best and least?
  ‣ Are South Africans getting poorer or richer?

See *data*

stem and leaf plot   A *stem and leaf plot* is a way of recording information (statistical data) using the first digit of a number (for example, the 2 in 25) as the stem and the last digit as the leaf (for example, the 5 in 25). It is a way of organising information relating to the number of entries in a particular group.

• Numbers to be organised in the *stem and leaf plot*:
18, 19, 17, 23, 25, 28, 29, 20, 25, 34, 35, 32, 37, 36, 33, 34, 32, 40, 42, 55

stem	leaves
1	8 9 7
②	3 ⑤ 8 9 0 5
3	4 5 2 7 6 3 4 2
4	0 2
5	5

sterling   *Sterling* is a name that refers to the money used in the United Kingdom (Great Britain). It is most often used in the phrase 'pounds *sterling*', which means 'British pounds'.

straight angle   A *straight angle* is an angle of 180° (half a revolution).

See *revolution*

straight edge   A *straight edge* is a length of wood, metal or plastic used to rule straight lines, or test whether a line drawn on a page is really straight.

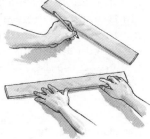

See *straight line*

straight line   A *straight line* is a line that has no curves or corners.

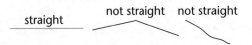

straight   not straight   not straight

See *line*

subdivision   A *subdivision* is a further division of something that has already been divided.

• The farm was divided into three smaller farms, one for each of Mr Mtimkulu's sons. One of these smaller farms was then further *subdivided* into ten plots of land, each big enough to build a small house.

• First divide the shape into quarters. Then *subdivide* each quarter into thirds.

subject of a formula   The *subject of a formula* is the variable in the formula that will be calculated when all the other values have been substituted into the formula. The *subject of the formula* is usually written on the left side of the equal sign, and the rest of the formula is rearranged to be written on the right side of the equal sign.

• In the formula $y = mx + c$, y is the *subject of the formula*. To make m the *subject of the formula*, rearrange the equation so that m is alone on the left side of the equal sign:

$$y = mx + c$$
$$mx + c = y$$
$$mx + c - c = y - c$$
$$mx = y - c$$
$$m = \frac{y - c}{x}$$

Now m is the *subject of the formula*. This process is called changing the *subject of the formula*.

See *formula; variable*

subset   A *subset* is a set of some of the elements that form part of a bigger set. If A is the big set of elements and B is the *subset* that contains only some of the elements in A, then B is a *subset* of A. This is written as $B \subset A$.

• In the three sets A, B and C where
A = {all numbers from 1 to 100}
B = {all even numbers from 2 to 100}
C = {4, 6, 8},
$B \subset A$, $C \subset B$ and $C \subset A$.

See *element of a set; set*

substitute, substitution   To *substitute* means to replace one thing with another thing. *Substitution* is the process of replacing the letters in a formula (equation) with numbers.

- In football games, if one player on the field is injured, the coach can *substitute* another player from the team.
- Use *substitution* to calculate the area of a rectangle when:
  a. $l = 12$ cm, $b = 7$ cm
  b. $l = 5,5$ cm, $b = 2$ cm
  Solution:
  a. Area $= l \times b = 12 \times 7 = 84$ cm^2
  b. Area $= l \times b = 5,5 \times 2 = 11$ cm^2

See *equation; formula*

subtend an angle   To *subtend an angle* means to form an angle at a point. When you look at an object such as a tree, the *angle subtended* at your eye is the angle formed by imagining two lines drawn from the top and bottom of the tree to your eye.

In geometry, when lines are drawn to join points on a circle, the lines *subtend* angles at the circumference of the circle.

- When the two lines AP and BP are drawn joining the three points A, B and P on this circle, then the *angle APB is subtended* by the chord AB or by the arc AB.

- All the angles formed on one side of a chord of a circle are equal to each other.

See *chord; circle*

subtract, subtraction   To *subtract* means to take one number (quantity) away from another number (quantity). This arithmetic operation is called *subtraction*. *Subtraction* is defined as the difference between two numbers. The sign for *subtraction* is '−', also called the minus sign.

- Use *subtraction* to find the difference between 800 and 450.
  Solution: $800 - 450 = 350$
  So the difference between 800 and 450 is 350.

See *addition; arithmetic*

sum   The *sum* of two or more numbers is their total value. The *sum* is calculated by adding the numbers together.

- Find the *sum* of 23, 4, 130 and 2 000.
  Solution:
  $23 + 4 + 130 + 2\,000 = 2\,157$.
  So the *sum* of these four numbers is 2 157.

See *addition*

summarise   To *summarise* something means to state its main points in a shorter form. In mathematics, formulae are often used to *summarise* the rules for calculating things.

- To calculate the area A of a triangle, you must multiply the base b by the height h, and divide the answer by 2. This method is *summarised* in the formula $A = \frac{1}{2}bh$.

supplementary angles   *Supplementary angles* are two or more angles that add up to 180°.

- The angles that form a straight line are *supplementary angles*.

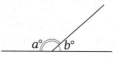

- The co-interior angles on one side of a transversal between two parallel lines are *supplementary angles*.

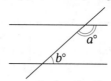

- The opposite *angles* of a cyclic quadrilateral are *supplementary*.

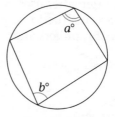

See *angle; co-interior angles; cyclic quadrilateral*

surd, surd form   A *surd* is a root of a number that cannot be expressed exactly as a decimal number with a finite number of places. It is an irrational number, and is usually written in *surd form* – that is, using the root symbol instead of writing out part of the decimal number.

- The cube root of 2 is an irrational number. It is usually written in *surd form* as $\sqrt[3]{2}$.

See *cube root*

surface   A *surface* is an exterior (outside) face of an object. The flat faces of a solid are all *surfaces*. Any flat area such as a floor or the top of a table is also called a *surface*.

- The cuboid has six *surfaces*. The sphere has only one *surface*.

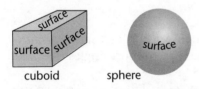

cuboid   sphere

See *face; solid*

surface area   The *surface area* of a solid is the total area of all its exterior surfaces.

- Look at this cylinder:

surface area of a closed cylinder = $h \times 2\pi r + 2\pi r^2$

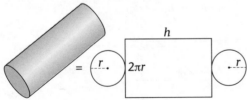

symbol   A *symbol* is any sign that is used to express an idea. Mathematics uses many *symbols* to express instructions, values and properties of numbers and shapes.

- Here are some mathematical *symbols* that are often used:
  - $+$ *symbol* for addition
  - $-$ *symbol* for subtraction
  - $\times$ *symbol* for multiplication
  - $\div$ *symbol* for division

- π *symbol* for the irrational number pi (3,1415826…)
- $\sqrt{\ }$ *symbol* for the square root of a number
- $\subset$ *symbol* for 'is a subset of'

symmetry, symmetrical   *Symmetry* is a property of certain shapes. Shapes that have *symmetry* can be reflected and turned to fit onto themselves. The more ways they can do this, the more *symmetry* they have. Shapes with *symmetry* are called *symmetrical* shapes.

Plane (flat) shapes have two kinds of *symmetry*:

- When a shape can be reflected onto itself about a line (the line of *symmetry*), it has line *symmetry*. Some shapes have more than one line of *symmetry*.
- When a shape can be rotated (turned) about a point through an angle of less than 360° to fit onto itself, it has rotational *symmetry*.

Solids can have planes of *symmetry*, and also rotational *symmetry*.

- The butterfly has one line of *symmetry*.

- The flower has three lines of *symmetry* and also rotational *symmetry* about its centre of order 5, because $\frac{1}{5}$ of a turn will fit the flower onto itself.

See *line of symmetry*

system   A *system* is any method of working or organising things, according to a set of rules.

- The metric *system* is a collection of measuring units that are organised as multiples of certain standard units of mass, length and capacity.

See *metric system*

T

table (data) A *table* is a way of organising information (data) so that it is easy to find the separate facts and figures in the *table*. A *table* usually has horizontal rows and vertical columns. The separate squares in the *table* are called 'cells'. Each cell contains one piece of information.

Province	State schools	Independent schools	Farm schools
Eastern Cape	6 100	900	4 600
Free State	2 450	300	1 500
Gauteng	1 800	400	300
KwaZulu-Natal	5 600	300	600
Limpopo	4 200	250	300
Mpumalanga	1 700	200	500
North West	2 200	100	500
Northern Cape	450	100	150
Western Cape	1 300	100	450

(Source: *South Africa at a Glance, 2003–2004*)

See *column; data; row*

table (multiplication) See *multiplication table*

tablespoon A *tablespoon* is a large spoon that is also a measuring unit used in cooking. 1 *tablespoon* is taken to be 12,5 millilitres of a liquid or solid ingredient.

tabulate, tabulation To *tabulate* information means to arrange the separate facts, numbers, etc. in the form of a table. This kind of *tabulation* is a useful way to organise information.
- Sibusiso uses a computer program to *tabulate* all his expenses for the month.

See *table (data)*

take away To *take away* a number means to subtract it from another number.
- If you *take away* 12 from 35, what do you get?
  Solution: 35 − 12 = 23

See *subtract*

tally A *tally* is a method of checking off (counting) a number of items by making a mark for each item counted. *Tallies* are often done in groups of five. Four lines are drawn for items 1 to 4, and then the fifth item is shown with a mark through the other four marks. This makes it easy to add up the groups of *tally* marks.
- The table shows the *tally* of the different colour shirts in a shop.

Colour of shirt	Tally	Frequency
Yellow	⦀⦀ ⦀⦀ ⎮⎮	12
Orange	⦀⦀ ⦀⦀ ⦀⦀ ⎮⎮⎮	18
Red	⦀⦀ ⎮⎮⎮⎮	9

See *table (data)*

tangent A *tangent* is a straight line that touches a curve at only one point.
- The *tangent* to the curve touches the curve at S.

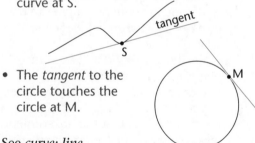

- The *tangent* to the circle touches the circle at M.

See *curve; line*

tangram A *tangram* is a Chinese puzzle made up of seven shapes that form a square. The shapes can be combined in many ways to make pictures of other objects.

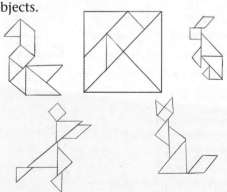

tape measure   A *tape measure* is a piece of tape made of metal, plastic or cloth, that is calibrated (marked off) in measuring units of length such as millimetres, centimetres and metres. It can be laid along the length of any object to measure the object's length.

- Builders, dressmakers and designers are some of the people who use *tape measures* in their work.

See *length*

tax   A *tax* is an amount of money that the government takes from people in the country, every time they do something like earn money, buy goods in a shop, buy a house, etc. *Taxes* are what the government uses to pay for all the public services that people use (such as roads, hospitals and schools) and to pay all the salaries of the people who work for government departments.

- These are some of the *taxes* that a person living in South African has to pay:
  - income *tax* – *tax* on the wage or salary you earn
  - value-added *tax* (VAT) – *tax* on the goods that you buy in a shop
  - transfer duty – *tax* that you pay if you buy a house or other property
  - estate duty – *tax* that the government takes on any money and property you own when you die, if it is over a certain value.

Tax rates for individuals: 2008/2009 tax year		
Taxable income (R)	**Rates of tax**	
0–122 000	18% of each R1	
122 001–195 000	R21 960 + 25%	of the amount above R122 000
195 001–270 000	R40 210 + 30%	of the amount above R195 000
270 001–380 000	R62 710 + 35%	of the amount above R270 000
380 001–490 000	R101 210 + 38%	of the amount above R380 000
490 001 and above	R143 010 + 40%	of the amount above R490 000
Rebates of tax		
Primary	R8 280	
Additional (persons 65 and older)	R5 040	
Tax threshold		
Below age 65	R46 000	
Age 65 and over	R74 000	

See *per cent; percentage*

teaspoon   A *teaspoon* is the small spoon that you use to stir drinks in a cup or mug. It is also a measuring unit used in cooking. 1 *teaspoon* is taken to be 5 millilitres of liquid or solid ingredients that are mixed together to make the food.

- To make hot chocolate, mix 4 *teaspoons* (20 ml) of chocolate powder into a mug of boiling water or hot milk.

See *millilitre*

tens   *Tens* are groups of ten units: 10, 20, 30, 40, ..., 170, 180, ..., 5 030, 5040, 5050, ...

10, 20, 30, ...

tenth   A *tenth* is a fraction that is equal to one part out of ten equal parts. Ten *tenths* are equal to one whole: $\frac{10}{10} = 1$.

- Sarah gave $\frac{1}{10}$ of the money to Loyiso and $\frac{9}{10}$ to Timothy.

See *fraction*

term   In a polynomial expression, a *term* is one part of the expression, separated from the other parts by a (+) or (–) sign. In a sequence, each member of the sequence is called a *term* of the sequence. The general *term* of the sequence is the algebraic expression that gives the rule for finding any *term* in the sequence.

- The polynomial $12x^2 + 30x + 7$ has three *terms*.
- In the sequence 5, 8, 11, 14, 17, ..., $3n + 2$, ... the first *term* is 5, the fourth *term* is 14, and the general *term* is $3n + 2$.

See *algebraic expression; polynomial; sequence*

terminating decimal   A *terminating decimal* is a number that can be written as a decimal with only a finite number of places. To 'terminate' means to end at an exact place. Decimals that do not terminate are irrational numbers such as

$\sqrt{2}$ and π, and recurring decimals in which the same digit or group of digits appears again and again.

- Examples of *terminating decimals*:

$$\frac{3}{5} = 0,6$$

$$\frac{7}{8} = 0,875$$

$$\frac{17}{625} = 0,0272$$

See *decimal; irrational number; recurring decimal*

tessellate, tessellation   When a set of shapes can be fitted together in a repeating pattern without leaving any gaps (spaces) between the shapes, we say that the shapes *tessellate*, and the pattern they form is called a *tessellation*.

- Tiles and bricks are often used to form *tessellations*.

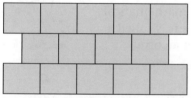

- In nature, a honeycomb is a set of *tessellated* shapes.

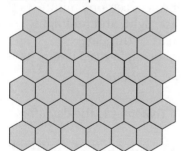

See *pattern; shape*

test   A *test* is a method of finding out how a substance behaves, or how a person performs. Scientists use *tests* to find out how different materials behave when they are heated, cooled, or changed in other ways. Teachers use *tests* to find out whether learners know how to do the activities they have studied at school.

- When a new car model is designed, the designers do many *tests* to find out what will happen to the car if it crashes.

tetrahedron   A *tetrahedron* is a polyhedron with four faces that are all triangular in shape. A *tetrahedron* is sometimes called a triangular-based pyramid. The base of the pyramid is a triangle, and the three other triangular faces meet at a point.

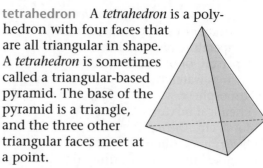

See *polyhedron; triangle*

theorem   A *theorem* is an important mathematical fact that can be proved in a step-by-step argument.

- Pythagoras' *theorem* is a famous mathematical *theorem*. It states that the square on the hypotenuse of a right-angled triangle is equal to the sum of the squares on the other two sides of the triangle.

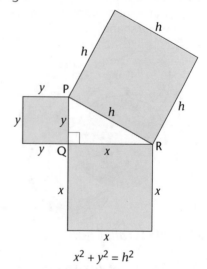

$$x^2 + y^2 = h^2$$

- If you split a quadrilateral into two triangles as shown, you can calculate the angle sum:

Angle sum = $a + b + c + d + e + f$
but $a + b + c = 180°$ and $d + e + f = 180°$.
So the angle sum = $180° + 180° = 360°$.
$\therefore$ Angle sum of a quadrilateral = $360°$.

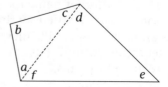

thermometer   A *thermometer* is an instrument used to measure the temperature (level of heat) of a person, or of a substance such as water, the atmosphere, a chemical mixture, food, etc. *Thermometers* are calibrated (marked off) in measuring units such as degrees Celsius, degrees Fahrenheit or Kelvin (a measuring unit used by scientists).

See *Celsius; Fahrenheit*

three-dimensional   A *three-dimensional* shape is a shape that has length, breadth and height. The abbreviation '3-D' is often used for *three-dimensional*. All the objects we see around us are *three-dimensional* objects.
- These fruits are examples of *three-dimensional* shapes.

See *breadth; height; length*

threes   *Threes* are groups of three things, or three consecutive numbers (for example 1, 2, 3 or 13, 14, 15).
- The class is divided into *threes* for this activity.
- It is easy to count in *threes* if you know the multiplication table for 3.

tiling   *Tiling* is another name for a tessellation. It refers to the way that shapes can be laid down like tiles, to form a repeating pattern that covers a surface without any gaps.

See *tessellate; tessellation*

times   The word *times* is sometimes used to mean multiplication. A '*times* table' is a multiplication table. A statement such as '3 *times* 2' means '3 multiplied by 2'. *Times* comes from the fact that when you multiply a number, you are really adding it to itself a given number of times.
- 12 *times* 5 means 12 added to itself 5 *times*: $12 + 12 + 12 + 12 + 12 = 60$. This repeated addition is the same as multiplication: $12 \times 5 = 60$.

See *multiplication*

tip   The *tip* of a shape is the pointed end of the shape. In everyday language this point is sometimes called a *tip*. In mathematical language it is called a vertex or a corner.

See *vertex*

today   *Today* is this day on which you are reading this dictionary. Everything that happens between one minute past midnight last night, and midnight tonight, is part of this day.
- *Today* I am going to clean up my room.

See *tomorrow; yesterday*

tomorrow   *Tomorrow* is the day after today.
- If I clean up my room today, my mother promised to take me to the beach *tomorrow*.

See *today; yesterday*

ton, tonne   A *ton* or *tonne* is the biggest unit of mass in the metric system and the imperial system. 1 metric *tonne* is equal to 1 000 kilograms. A *ton* in the imperial system has almost the same mass as a metric *tonne*.
- A full-grown African elephant has a mass of about 6 *tonnes*.

See *imperial units; metric system*

top The *top* of a shape is the highest part of the shape – the part that is furthest away from the base. The *top* position in a space is the point that is furthest away from the ground.

• The *top* of a pyramid is a point.

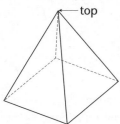

• It is hard to reach the books on the *top* shelf in a bookshop.

See *base; bottom*

torus A *torus* is a mathematical name for a round shape with a hole in the middle. It comes from the Greek word for an anchor ring.

• A life belt and a doughnut have the shape of a *torus*.

total A *total* is the quantity that is obtained by adding different amounts together. It is the sum of all the parts of an arithmetic calculation.

• To calculate the *total* cost of the holiday, you should add the air fares, the price of a hotel, the money you will spend on food there, the cost of sightseeing tours, and the cost of buying presents for your friends at home.

• If you add 20, 35, 57 and 92 you get a *total* of 204.

$$\begin{array}{r} 20 \\ 35 \\ 57 \\ \underline{92} \\ \text{Total: } \underline{204} \end{array}$$

See *sum*

total surface area The *total surface area* of a solid figure is the sum of the areas of all the faces of the solid, measured in square units.

• The *total surface area* of this cuboid is:

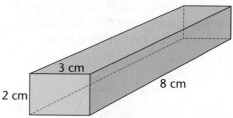

Total surface area = 6 faces
= 2 × (*l* × *b*) + 2(*b* × *h*) + 2(*l* × *h*)
= 2 × (8 × 3) + 2(3 × 2) + 2(8 × 2) cm²
= 48 + 12 + 32
= 92 cm²

See *area; square unit; surface*

trace To *trace* something such as a shape or a picture means to copy it by this method:

• Place a piece of transparent (see-through) paper on top of the picture – this is called *tracing paper*.

• With a pen, draw over all the lines of the picture on the tracing paper.

• Turn the tracing paper over and rub the back of it with a soft pencil until you have covered all the lines you drew.

- Place the tracing paper on a clean sheet of paper, with the picture side on top, and draw over the picture lines with a pen or hard pencil.

The picture that you copied will now be shown on the paper under the tracing paper.

transformation To transform something means to change it in some way. A *transformation* is the method that makes the change happen. The *transformation* may change a set of numbers, or change a set of points (a shape).

- A *transformation* that changes a set of numbers is expressed as a mapping, or rule, that you apply, to change the set of numbers into different numbers. For example, the *transformation* $n \to 7 - n$ means 'transform each number n into the number $7 - n$'. This *transformation* will change a 'magic triangle' containing the numbers 1 to 6 into a different magic triangle with the same numbers.

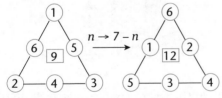

- There are many kinds of geometric *transformations*. Some of them are:
  - translations, which move an object to a new position without changing its shape, size or direction
  - rotations, which turn an object about its axis of symmetry
  - reflections, which reflect an object's mirror image along its axis of symmetry

- enlargements, which increase the size of the object without changing its shape or direction.

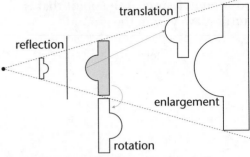

See *mapping; reflection; rotation; translation*

transformation geometry *Transformation geometry* is the branch of mathematics that studies the transformations that can be made to shapes and objects.

translation A *translation* is a type of geometrical transformation. When a shape is transformed by sliding it to a new position without turning it, it is said to be *translated* to the new position.

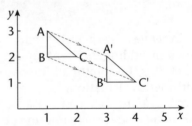

See *transformation*

transparent, transparency An object is *transparent* if you can see through it. A *transparency* is a sheet of see-through writing paper that can be used with an overhead projector, to show information on the wall of a room.

transpose To *transpose* two shapes or numbers means to make them change places with each other.

- If you *transpose* the digits in the number 76 you get the number 67.

See *digit*

transversal A *transversal* is a line drawn across two or more parallel lines. A *transversal* forms equal angles with the parallel lines, such as corresponding angles (for example *x* and *y* in the diagram) and alternate angles (for example *p* and *x* in the diagram).

See *alternate angles; corresponding angles; parallel*

trapezium or trapezoid A *trapezium* is a quadrilateral with one pair of opposite sides parallel. It is sometimes called a *trapezoid* shape.

- This building is made up of *trapezium* shapes.

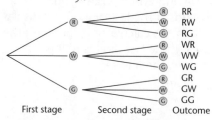

See *parallel; quadrilateral*

tree diagram A *tree diagram* is a diagram that is used to show all the possible outcomes (results) and probabilities when two or more events are combined in a statistical analysis.

- If you have a box with two red, two green and two white balls in it, and you choose two balls without looking, you can use a *tree diagram* to work out all the possible colour combinations of the balls that you picked. This shows there are nine possible outcomes, a $\frac{1}{9}$ probability.

First stage   Second stage   Outcome

See *event; outcome; probability*

trial A *trial* is an experiment to test whether or not a new invention works.

- When new medicines are invented, they go through many *trials* on animals and people before they can be used to treat sick people.

triangle A *triangle* is a closed shape formed from three straight lines. 'Tri-' means three. A *triangle* has three interior angles. It is the simplest polygon. There are four types of *triangles*: equilateral, isosceles, right-angled and scalene.

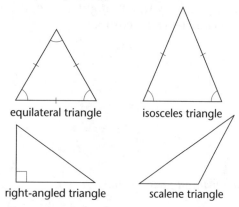

equilateral triangle   isosceles triangle

right-angled triangle   scalene triangle

See *angle; equilateral triangle; isosceles triangle; right-angled triangle; scalene triangle*

triangle numbers or triangular numbers
The *triangle numbers* are the numbers in the sequence 1, 3, 6, 10, 15, 21, 28, 36, ..., $\frac{1}{2}n(n + 1)$, ... where *n* is any whole number.

They are called *triangle numbers* because they correspond to the number of dots required to build triangular shapes.

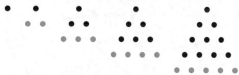

Each new triangle is formed from the previous triangle by adding a new base with one more dot than the base before it. Each *triangle number* is the sum of consecutive whole numbers. For example, the fifth *triangle number* is
$1 + 2 + 3 + 4 + 5 = 15$.

See *sequence; triangle*

triangular prism A *triangular prism* is a solid whose sides are parallelograms and whose ends are equal and parallel triangles.

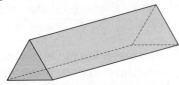

See *parallelogram; prism; triangle*

triangular pyramid A *triangular pyramid* is a pyramid with a triangular base. It is also called a tetrahedron.

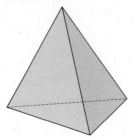

See *pyramid; tetrahedron*

triangulate, triangulation To *triangulate* means to find the position or value of a point by measuring it in relation to two other points that can be joined with the unknown point to form a triangle shape.
- *Triangulation* is a method used to survey the land and draw maps that show where different places on the land are.

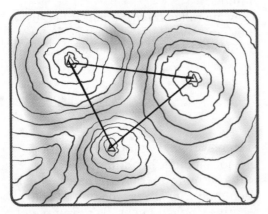

See *triangle*

trigonometry *Trigonometry* is the branch of mathematics used in land surveying and navigation at sea. It is also used to study the relationships between the lengths of the sides of triangles and their angles, and the ways in which waves move.

trillion A *trillion* is a million million, or 10^{12}.
- We write one *trillion* as 1 with 12 zeroes after it: 1 000 000 000 000

See *million*

trinomial A *trinomial* is a polynomial with three terms. 'Tri-' means three.
- Examples of *trinomials* are:
  $10x^2 + 3x - 45$
  $7xy + 98y^2z + x^3z^2$

See *polynomial; term*

true A mathematical statement is *true* if it gives the correct solution, or accurately describes a shape or number, or can be proved by means of correct reasoning.
- The statement $3 + 3 = 6$ is *true*.
- The statement $3 + 3 = 7$ is not *true*. (It is false.)

truncate If a long number with many digits is cut off at any digit, without rounding off the number, it is called *truncating* the number.
- Electronic calculators carry out calculations to a higher degree of accuracy than they can show in their display window. Some calculators round the answer to fit the number of places available in the display. Other calculators just cut off the digits at the end when there is no more room in the display, without rounding the number.
- Try dividing 2 by 3, using your calculator. If the last digit in the display is 7 then the calculator is rounding the answer. If the last digit is 6, it is *truncating* the answer.

See *round off*

truncated shape   A *truncated shape* is a solid shape such as a cone or a pyramid that has had its top cut off.

- Lampshades are often in the shape of *truncated cones.*

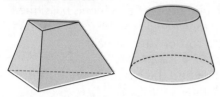

See *cone; pyramid; shape*

trundle wheel   *See* metre wheel

turn   To *turn* means to move in a curved direction. A *turn* is a curving movement. A full *turn* is a movement through a complete circle (360°). A *half turn* is 180° and a *quarter turn* is 90°.

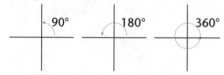

See *rotation*

twice   *Twice* means 'two times'.

- James went to the shop *twice* today. The first time he bought a morning news-paper. The second time he bought a pie for lunch.

two-dimensional   A *two-dimensional* shape is a flat shape that has length and breadth but no height. The abbreviation '2-D' is often used for *two-dimensional*.

- A Cartesian plane is a *two-dimensional* shape:

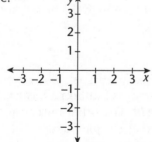

- All polygons are *two-dimensional* shapes.

See *breadth; length*

two-way table   A *two-way table* is a table that shows how two sets of statistical data can be combined to give many possible outcomes.

- A distance table combines distances between many different places into one table. The distance between any two places can be read off from the table.

	Bloemfontein	Cape Town	Durban	East London	Gaborone	Johannesburg	Kimberley
Bloemfontein	–	1 004	634	584	622	398	177
Cape Town	1 004	–	1 753	1 079	1 501	1 402	969
Colesburg	226	778	860	488	848	624	292
Durban	634	1 753	–	674	979	557	811
East London	584	1 079	674	–	1 206	982	780
Gaborone	622	1 501	979	1 206	–	358	538
George	773	438	1 319	645	1 361	1 171	762

See *data*

U

uneven number An *uneven number* is a number that cannot be divided exactly by 2, without a remainder. *Uneven number* is another name for 'odd number'.
- The first ten *uneven numbers* are 1, 3, 5, 7, 9, 11, 13, 15, 17, 19.
- $67 \div 2 = 33$ remainder 1. Therefore 67 is an *uneven number*.

See *even numbers; odd numbers*

ungrouped data *Ungrouped data* are collections of raw data (number facts) that have not been grouped into classes or categories.
- The test results for the whole class are written on this list as *ungrouped data*. They have not yet been arranged into different categories, for example 0–20%, 21–40%, and so on.

Class list	
Andrews, André	81%
Dondole, Vuyo	62%
Galant, Marco	55%
Gomba, Kazi	94%
Jenkins, Philip	46%
Molepo, Simpiwe	79%
Stanfliet, Jerome	51%
Wright, Jessica	65%

See *data*

union of sets The *union of sets* is the combination of the elements in all the sets into a new set, the *union set*. The symbol for a *union of sets* is ∪.
- The *union of the two sets* A = {2, 3, 5, 7, 11} and B = {2, 5, 8, 11, 14} is the set A ∪ B = {2, 3, 5, 7, 8, 11, 14}

See *element of a set; intersection of sets; set*

unit The smallest natural number, 1, is called a *unit*. The numbers 1 to 9 are called the units in the base 10 place value system.

See *base of a number*

unit fractions Fractions with a numerator of 1 are called *unit fractions*.

unitary method The *unitary method* is a method for finding the total value (cost) of a group of items by first finding the cost of one of the items.
- If 3 tennis balls cost R5,52 and you want to find the cost of 5 tennis balls, the *unitary method* can be used. First find the cost of 1 tennis ball: R5,52 ÷ 3 = R1,84
- Then find the cost of 5 tennis balls: R1,84 × 5 = R9,20

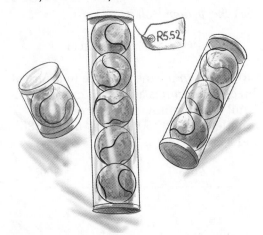

unitary ratio A *unitary ratio* is a ratio in which the first number in the ratio is 1. Any ratio of the form $m : n$ can be written in the form $1 : k$ by dividing both values in the ratio by m. A ratio in the form $1 : k$ is a *unitary ratio*.
- To convert the ratio 3 : 15 to a *unitary ratio*, divide both values by 3: 3 : 15 is the same as the *unitary ratio* 1 : 5.
- To convert the ratio 2 : 7 to a *unitary ratio*, divide both values by 2: 2 : 7 is the same as the *unitary ratio* 1 : 3,5.

See *ratio*

units of measurement Every system of measurement is built on a basic *unit of measurement*. The other measuring units are formed as simple fractions or multiples of this unit.
- The basic unit of length in the metric system is the metre. This unit is divided into 100 equal parts to give a centimetre

or 1 000 equal parts to give a millimetre. It is multiplied by 1 000 to give a kilometre.

10 mm = 1 cm
100 cm = 1 m
1 000 m = 1 km

See *metric system*

universal set   In a given situation the set of all elements being considered is called the *universal set*. The symbol for this set is ε. All the elements in all the smaller sets in this situation come from the *universal set* of elements.
In a Venn diagram, the *universal set* is usually drawn as a rectangle around all the other sets.

* The learners in Grade 9 at Zingisa Secondary School can be grouped in different sets according to their sports choices:
  A = {learners who play hockey}
  B = {learners who swim}
  C = {learners who play netball}
  D = {learners who play tennis}
  E = {learners who do not play any sport}
  The *universal set* in this situation is
  ε = {the set of all Grade 9 learners at Zinigisa Secondary School}. Sets A, B, C, D and E are all subsets of ε.

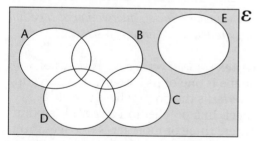

See *element of a set; set; subset; Venn diagram*

unknown number   An *unknown number* in an equation is a number whose value is not known. In an expression like $3x + 4$, x is the variable.

* In the equation $3x + 4 = 7$, x is the *unknown number*.

See *algebra; variable*

V

value   The *value* of an item is how important it is for the people who need or want it. The *value* of a mathematical expression is the total amount (quantity) of the expression, expressed as a number.

* Malusi's old coat has great *value* for him because it belonged to his grandfather, who died when he was a little boy.
* Calculate the *value* of the expression $3ab + 2b + c$, when $a = 4$, $b = 5$ and $c = 6$.
  Solution: $3ab + 2b + c = (3 \times 4 \times 5) + (2 \times 5) + 6 = 60 + 10 + 6 = 76$.
  So the *value* of the expression is 76, when $a = 4$, $b = 5$ and $c = 6$.

variable   A *variable* is a letter in an algebraic expression that can stand for many different numbers. To 'vary' means to change. The value of the whole expression will depend on the values that are chosen for each *variable* in the expression.

* The formula $v = u + at$ has four *variables*: v, u, a and t. The value of v will change for different values of the *variables* u, a and t.

See *constant; dependent variable; independent variable*

varies directly as   When two variables are related by an equation of the form $y = kx$, where k is a constant, then y varies (changes) *directly as* x varies. This means that as the value of x increases (gets bigger), the value of y will also increase.

* When a ball is dropped from a height x onto a hard surface it will bounce to a height y where $y = kx$. This can be shown on a graph as a straight line.

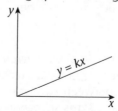

See *direct proportion; linear*

varies inversely as   When two variables are related by an equation of the form $y = \frac{k}{x}$, where k is a constant, then y varies (changes) *inversely as x* varies. This means that as the value of x increases (gets bigger), the value of y will decrease (get smaller).

- The pressure P of a gas at constant temperature *varies inversely as* its volume V varies. The relation between P and V is given as $P = \frac{k}{V}$. The graph of this relation is a hyperbola.

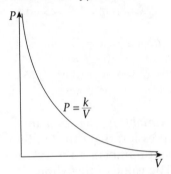

See *hyperbola; inverse proportion*

VAT   VAT is the abbreviation for value-added tax. It is a tax that the govern-ment charges on most of the items that you buy in the shops. VAT is calculated as a percentage of the selling price of the item. In South Africa at present the VAT rate is 14%. This means that 14% of the amount that you pay for anything you buy, goes to the government and not to the shop owner (remember that some food items are excempt from VAT).

See *per cent; percentage; tax*

velocity   The *velocity* of an object is the rate at which it changes its position with time. It is defined by the object's direction of travel as well as its speed.

- The *velocity* of an aeroplane may be given as 900 km/h on a bearing of 072°.

See *bearing*

Venn diagram   A *Venn diagram* is a diagram where regions are used to show the relation between two or more sets of elements. Each set is shown as a circle, and the universal set (ε) that contains all the sets is shown as a rectangle. The region where two or more sets overlap shows the intersection of the sets – it contains the elements that are common to all the sets. *Venn diagrams* are named after John Venn (1834–1923), a British mathematician.

- In this *Venn diagram*, the region inside the rectangle shows the natural numbers from 1 to 20. It represents the universal set ε = {natural numbers from 1 to 20}.
- The region inside the blue circle contains all the even numbers between 1 and 15.
- The region inside the black circle contains all the even numbers between 1 and 10 and uneven numbers between 10 and 20.
- The region where the two circles overlap represents the intersection of these two sets: {the set of even numbers between 1 and 10}.

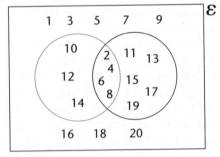

See *element of a set; intersection of sets; line of symmetry; set; universal set*

vertex (plural: vertices)   A *vertex* of a shape is one of its corners. In a polygon, a *vertex* is the point where two sides meet. In a polyhedron a *vertex* is a point where three or more faces or edges meet. The pointed end of a cone is called its *vertex*.

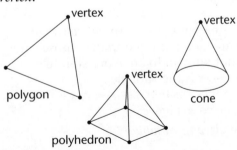

See *edge; face; polygon; polyhedron*

vertical, vertical line   The *vertical* direction is the direction in which an object will fall if it is dropped. It corresponds to the direction of gravity. A *vertical line* is a line that meets a horizontal line at a right angle (90°).

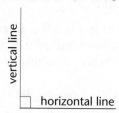

See *horizontal*

vertically opposite angles   *Vertically opposite angles* are the angles that are directly opposite each other when two lines cross at a point. There are two pairs of *vertically opposite angles* wherever two lines cross. *Vertically opposite angles* are equal to each other.
- In the diagram, there are two pairs of *vertically opposite angles*: $a = b$ and $x = y$.

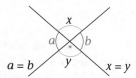

See *angle; line*

volume   The *volume* of a solid shape is the amount of space that it occupies. It is measured by the number of unit cubes that are needed to fill the space. In the metric system, common units for measuring *volume* are cubic millimetres (mm^3), cubic centimetres (cm^3) and cubic metres (m^3).
- A cuboid measuring 4 cm by 2 cm by 2 cm can be filled with 16 unit cubes. There are two layers of cubes, each with $4 \times 2 = 8$ cubes. Each unit cube has a *volume* of 1 cubic centimetre (cm^3) so the cuboid has a *volume* of 16 cm^3.

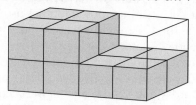

See *capacity; cube; solid; unit*

vulgar fraction   See *common fraction*

W

week, weekday, weekend   A *week* is a period of 7 consecutive days (days that follow one after another). In most societies, 5 or 6 of these are days on which people go to school and to work. These days are called *weekdays*. One or 2 of the days of the *week* are days for rest, prayer and entertainment – these days are called the *weekend*. There are 4 *weeks* and 2 or 3 days in one calendar month (30 or 31 days). There are 52 *weeks* in one year.

- The calendar that most countries use gives these names to the days of the *week*: Monday, Tuesday, Wednesday, Thursday, Friday, Saturday, Sunday. Monday to Friday are *weekdays* (working days), and Saturday and Sunday are the *weekend* days. Friday, Saturday or Sunday is the day of prayer in different religions.

See *day; month; year*

weigh   To *weigh* an object means to measure its mass.

- The doctor or nurse *weighs* patients to check if they have a healthy body mass for their height and age.

See *mass*

weight   The *weight* of an object is the force of gravity on the object. This can differ from place to place. The same object on the moon's surface would *weigh* only $\frac{1}{6}$ of its *weight* on the Earth, because the gravitational force of the moon is $\frac{1}{6}$ as strong as the gravitational force on Earth. The *weight* of the same object in a satellite orbiting the Earth would be 0, because the gravitational force in space is so small that it is almost equivalent to 0.

west   *West* is one of the four cardinal (main) points of the compass. It is the direction opposite east on the compass.

- The Sun sets in the west, wherever you are on Earth.

See *compass; east; north; south*

whole   Something is *whole* if it contains all its parts. A *whole* amount is an amount from which nothing has been taken away.

- The *whole* class must stay behind after school to clean the classroom.
- The *whole* cake is big enough to feed 10 people.

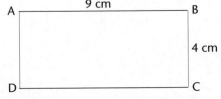

- Lily spent the *whole* year, from January to December, training for the athletics competition in December.

See *fraction*

whole number   A *whole number* is any number from the set of counting numbers $\mathbb{R} = \{1, 2, 3, \dots\}$ *Whole numbers* can also be described as positive integers. The number 0 is sometimes included in the set of whole numbers.

- Examples of whole numbers are 5, 20, 914, 1 000 350.

See *counting numbers; integer*

wide, width   To describe how *wide* a shape is, you measure the shorter side of the shape. This gives the *width* of the shape. *Width* is another name for 'breadth'.

- The rectangle ABCD is 9 cm long and 4 cm *wide*. Its *width* is 4 cm.

```
      9 cm
A ┌──────────┐ B
  │          │
  │          │ 4 cm
  │          │
D └──────────┘ C
```

See *breadth*

withdraw   To *withdraw* money from the bank means to take money out of a bank account.

- Every month Mazisi *withdraws* R500 from his savings account to pay for his monthly expenses.

See *bank account; deposit*

word problem   A *word problem* is a mathematical problem that is described using words instead of numbers. The first step in solving a *word problem* is usually to express the problem in the form of an expression with numbers and variables. This makes it possible to do the calculations that will give the solution to the problem.

- An example of a *word problem*:
  A local cinema complex has 800 seats divided into 3 theatres. There are 270 seats in Cine 1. Cine 2 has 150 more seats than Cine 3. How many seats are in Cine 2?

  Answer
  Let x = number of seats in Cine 3 (C3)
    C1 = Cine 1 = 270 seats
    C2 = Cine 2 = 150 + x

      C1 + C2 + C3 = 800 seats
  270 + (150 + x) + x = 800
         420 + 2x = 800
            2x = 800 − 420
            2x = 380
             x = 190

  If there are x = 190 seats in Cine 3, then Cine 2 has 150 + 190 = 340 seats

See *expression; variable*

work out   To *work out* the answer to a problem means to use mathematical methods (such as arithmetic and algebra) to calculate the solution to the problem.

See *calculate; solution*

wrong   A *wrong* statement is a statement that is not true. A *wrong* answer to a calculation is an answer that is incorrect, because a mistake has been made.

- A *wrong* statement:
  The Sun sets in the east.
- A *wrong* answer:
  10 + 10 = 100.

See *correct; right*

X

x-axis   The *x-axis* on a graph is the horizontal axis. The values along the *x-axis* are the *x*-values in an equation that is shown on the graph.

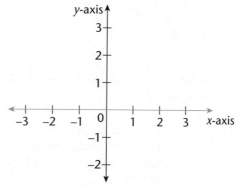

See *axis; graph; horizontal; y-axis*

Y

Z

yard   A *yard* is a unit of length in the imperial measuring system. One *yard* is equal to three feet, or 36 inches. One *yard* is approximately equal to 90 centimetres.

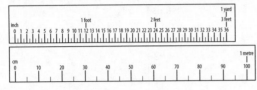

See *imperial units*

y-axis   The *y-axis* on a graph is the vertical axis. The values along the *y-axis* are the *y*-values in an equation that is shown on the graph.

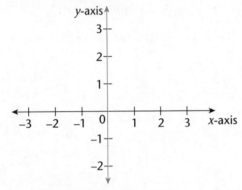

See *axis; graph; vertical; x-axis*

year   A *year* is a unit of time measurement. One *year* = 12 months = 52 weeks = 365 days = 8 760 hours = 525 600 minutes = 31 536 000 seconds.

• The oldest recorded age that a person has attained anywhere in the world is 122 *years*. It was the lifespan of Jeanne Calment of France (1875–1997) who was 122 years and 164 days old when she died.

See *leap year*

yesterday   *Yesterday* is the day before today.

• 'Today is my birthday. *Yesterday* I was 15. Today I am 16!'

See *today; tomorrow*

zero   *Zero* is the mathematical term for the concept of 'nothing'. The symbol for *zero* is 0. It is a place holder in our place value number system. It allows us to use the same digit, for example 4, to mean numbers of different size: 4, 40, 0,04, 4 000 000.

• *Zero* is the identity element for addition and subtraction. To add or subtract 0 from a number does not change the value of the number.
  For example:
  $3 + 0 = 3$
  $10 - 0 = 10$

• *Zero* is the number that separates the positive and negative numbers on a number line:

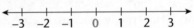

See *identity element; nil; nought; place value*

DIFFERENT CALENDARS

Islamic calendar	Months of the Indian Civil Calendar	Jewish calendar
Muharram	Caitra	Nisan
Rajab	Vaisakha	Iyar
Safar	Jyaistha	Sivan
Sha'ban	Aasadha	Tammuz
Rabi' al-awwal (Rabi' I)	Sravana	Av
Ramadan	Bhadra	Elul
Rabi' al-thani (Rabi' II)	Asvina	Tishri
Shawwal	Kartika	Cheshvan
Jumada al-awwal (Jumada I)	Agrahayana	Kislev
Dhu al-Qi'dah	Pausa	Tevet
Jumada al-thani (Jumada II)	Magha	Shevat
Dhu al-Hijjah	Phalguna	Adar I
		Adar II

MORSE CODE ALPHABET

A •—	N —•	0 —————
B —•••	O ———	1 •————
C —•—•	P •——•	2 ••———
D —••	Q ——•—	3 •••——
E •	R •—•	4 ••••—
F ••—•	S •••	5 •••••
G ——•	T —	6 —••••
H ••••	U ••—	7 ——•••
I ••	V •••—	8 ———••
J •———	W •——	9 ————•
K —•—	X —••—	Fullstop •—•—•—
L •—••	Y —•——	Comma ——••——
M ——	Z ——••	Query ••——••

ROMAN NUMERALS

1	I
2	II
3	III
4	IV
5	V
6	VI
7	VII
8	VIII
9	IX
10	X
11	XI
12	XII
15	XV
50	L
84	LXXXIV
90	XC
99	XCIX
100	C
1 002	MII
2 025	MMXXV

MULTIPLICATION TABLES

1 × 1 = 1	2 × 1 = 2	3 × 1 = 3	4 × 1 = 4
1 × 2 = 2	2 × 2 = 4	3 × 2 = 6	4 × 2 = 8
1 × 3 = 3	2 × 3 = 6	3 × 3 = 9	4 × 3 = 12
1 × 4 = 4	2 × 4 = 8	3 × 4 = 12	4 × 4 = 16
1 × 5 = 5	2 × 5 = 10	3 × 5 = 15	4 × 5 = 20
1 × 6 = 6	2 × 6 = 12	3 × 6 = 18	4 × 6 = 24
1 × 7 = 7	2 × 7 = 14	3 × 7 = 21	4 × 7 = 28
1 × 8 = 8	2 × 8 = 16	3 × 8 = 24	4 × 8 = 32
1 × 9 = 9	2 × 9 = 18	3 × 9 = 27	4 × 9 = 36
1 × 10 = 10	2 × 10 = 20	3 × 10 = 30	4 × 10 = 40
1 × 11 = 11	2 × 11 = 22	3 × 11 = 33	4 × 11 = 44
1 × 12 = 12	2 × 12 = 24	3 × 12 = 36	4 × 12 = 48
5 × 1 = 5	6 × 1 = 6	7 × 1 = 7	8 × 1 = 8
5 × 2 = 10	6 × 2 = 12	7 × 2 = 14	8 × 2 = 16
5 × 3 = 15	6 × 3 = 18	7 × 3 = 21	8 × 3 = 24
5 × 4 = 20	6 × 4 = 24	7 × 4 = 28	8 × 4 = 32
5 × 5 = 25	6 × 5 = 30	7 × 5 = 35	8 × 5 = 40
5 × 6 = 30	6 × 6 = 36	7 × 6 = 42	8 × 6 = 48
5 × 7 = 35	6 × 7 = 42	7 × 7 = 49	8 × 7 = 56
5 × 8 = 40	6 × 8 = 48	7 × 8 = 56	8 × 8 = 64
5 × 9 = 45	6 × 9 = 54	7 × 9 = 63	8 × 9 = 72
5 × 10 = 50	6 × 10 = 60	7 × 10 = 70	8 × 10 = 80
5 × 11 = 55	6 × 11 = 66	7 × 11 = 77	8 × 11 = 88
5 × 12 = 60	6 × 12 = 72	7 × 12 = 84	8 × 12 = 96
9 × 1 = 9	10 × 1 = 10	11 × 1 = 11	12 × 1 = 12
9 × 2 = 18	10 × 2 = 20	11 × 2 = 22	12 × 2 = 24
9 × 3 = 27	10 × 3 = 30	11 × 3 = 33	12 × 3 = 36
9 × 4 = 36	10 × 4 = 40	11 × 4 = 44	12 × 4 = 48
9 × 5 = 45	10 × 5 = 50	11 × 5 = 55	12 × 5 = 60
9 × 6 = 54	10 × 6 = 60	11 × 6 = 66	12 × 6 = 72
9 × 7 = 63	10 × 7 = 70	11 × 7 = 77	12 × 7 = 84
9 × 8 = 72	10 × 8 = 80	11 × 8 = 88	12 × 8 = 96
9 × 9 = 81	10 × 9 = 90	11 × 9 = 99	12 × 9 = 108
9 × 10 = 90	10 × 10 = 100	11 × 10 = 110	12 × 10 = 120
9 × 11 = 99	10 × 11 = 110	11 × 11 = 121	12 × 11 = 132
9 × 12 = 108	10 × 12 = 120	11 × 12 = 132	12 × 12 = 144

THE MULTIPLICATION SQUARE

×	1	2	3	4	5	6	7	8	9	10
1	1	2	3	4	5	6	7	8	9	10
2	2	4	6	8	10	12	14	16	18	20
3	3	6	9	12	15	18	21	24	27	30
4	4	8	12	16	20	24	28	32	36	40
5	5	10	15	20	25	30	35	40	45	50
6	6	12	18	24	30	36	42	48	54	60
7	7	14	21	28	35	42	49	56	63	70
8	8	16	24	32	40	48	56	64	72	80
9	9	18	27	36	45	54	63	72	81	90
10	10	20	30	40	50	60	70	80	90	100

CONVERSION TABLES: METRIC AND IMPERIAL

LENGTH		
Metric		**Imperial**
1 mm		0,03937 in
1 cm	10 mm	0,3937 in
1 m	100 cm	1,0936 yd
1 km	1 000 m	0,6214 miles
Imperial		**Metric**
1 in		2,54 cm
1 ft	12 in	0,3048 m
1 yd	3 ft	0,9144 m
1 mile	1 760 yd	1,6093 km
1 nautical mile	2 025.4 yd	1,835 km

CONVERSION TABLES: METRIC AND IMPERIAL (continued)

AREA		
Metric		**Imperial**
1 cm^2	100 mm^2	0,155 in^2
1 m^2	10 000 cm^2	1,1960 yd^2
1 ha	10 000 m^2	2,4711 acres
1 km^2	100 ha	0,3861 mile^2
Imperial		**Metric**
1 in^2		6,4516 cm^2
1 ft^2	144 in^2	0,0929 m^2
1 yd^2	9 ft^2	0,8361 m^2
1 acre	4 840 yd^2	4 046,9 m^2
1 mile^2	640 acres	2,59 km^2
MASS		
Metric		**Imperial**
1 mg		0,0154 grain
1 g	1 000 mg	0,0353 oz
1 kg	1 000 g	2,2046 lb
1 t	1 000 kg	0,9842 ton
Imperial		**Metric**
1 oz	437.5 grain	28,35 g
1 lb	16 oz	0,4536 kg
1 stone	14 lb	6,3503 kg
1 long ton	20 cwt	1,016 t
VOLUME		
Metric		**Imperial**
1 cm^3		0,061 in^3
1 dm^3	1 000 cm^3	0,0353 ft^3
1 ℓ	1 dm^3	1,76 pt
1 hl	100 ℓ	21,997 gallons
Imperial		**Metric**
1 in^3		16,387 cm^3
1 ft^3	1 728 in^3	0,0283 m^3
1 fluid oz		28,413 ml
1 pt	20 fluid oz	0,5683 ℓ
1 gallon	8 pt	4,5461 ℓ

(in = inch, yd = yard, ft = foot, oz = ounce, lb = pound; t = tonne; pt = pint)

SEVEN BASE UNITS OF THE SI SYSTEM

Unit	Symbol	Quantity measured
metre	m	length (distance)
second	s	time
kilogram	kg	mass
Ampere	A	electric current
Kelvin	K	temperature
candela	cd	light intensity
mole	mol	amount of substance

TEMPERATURE CONVERSION TABLE

°C	0	5	15	20	30	40	50	60	70	80	90	100
°F	32	41	59	68	86	104	122	140	158	176	194	212
K	273	278	288	293	303	313	323	333	343	353	363	373

CONVERSION TABLE FOR WOMEN'S CLOTHING SIZES

UK	10	12	14	16	18	20	22
EU	38	40	42	44	46	48	50
RSA	34	36	38	40	42	44	46

CONVERSION TABLE FOR SHOE SIZES

RSA	3	4	5	6	7	8	9	10	11	12
EU	36	37	38	39	41	42	43	44	46	47

12-HOUR AND 24-HOUR TIME

Morning		Afternoon/evening	
12-hour time	24-hour time	12-hour time	24-hour time
12 a.m. (midnight)	00:00	12 p.m. (noon)	12:00
1 a.m.	01:00	1 p.m.	13:00
2 a.m.	02:00	2 p.m.	14:00
3 a.m.	03:00	3 p.m.	15:00
4 a.m.	04:00	4 p.m.	16:00
5 a.m.	05:00	5 p.m.	17:00
6 a.m.	06:00	6 p.m.	18:00
7 a.m.	07:00	7 p.m.	19:00
8 a.m.	08:00	8 p.m.	20:00
9 a.m.	09:00	9 p.m.	21:00
10 a.m.	10:00	10 p.m.	22:00
11 a.m.	11:00	11 p.m.	23:00

FORMULAE FOR PLANE SHAPES AND SOLIDS

PLANE SHAPES			
Shape	**Diagram**	**Perimeter**	**Area**
Rectangle		$P = 2(l + b)$	$A = lb$
Square		$P = 4(s)$	$A = s^2$
Triangle		$P = a + b + c$ (where a, b and c are sides of the triangle)	$A = \frac{1}{2}bh$
Circle		$C = 2\pi r$ **or** $C = \pi d$	$A = \pi r^2$
Parallelogram		$P = 2(h + b)$	$A = bh$
Trapezium		$P = a + b + c + d$	$A = \frac{1}{2}$(sum of parallel sides) (perpendicular height) $A = \frac{(a + b)}{2} \times h$
Kite		$P = a + b + c + d$	$A = \frac{1}{2}$(product of the diagonals) $= \frac{1}{2}(f \times g)$
Rhombus		$P = 4s$	$A = sh$

SOLIDS

Shape	Diagram	Volume	Surface area
Cube		$V = s^3$	Area of six squares $= 6x^2$
Cuboid		$V = lbh$	Area of six rectangles $= 2(lh + hb + lb)$
Cylinder		$V = \pi r^2 h$	Area of two circles and area of curved surface $= 2\pi r^2 + 2\pi rh$ $= 2\pi r(r + h)$
Square-based pyramid		$V = \frac{1}{3}b^2 h$	Area of square base and area of four triangular faces $= b^2 + 4 \times \frac{1}{2}bh$ $= b^2 + 2bh$
Cone		$V = \frac{1}{3}\pi r^2 h$	Radius × slant height $A = \pi r^2 \times \pi rl$ $= \pi r(r + l)$
Sphere		$V = \frac{4}{3}\pi r^3$	Area of four circles $= 4\pi r^2$

(l = length, b = breadth, h = height, s = side, r = radius, d = diameter, diag. = diagonal line, l = slant height of cone)